# Black Flags of the Caribbean

# Black Flags of the Caribbean

## *How Trinidad Became an ISIS Hotspot*

Simon Cottee

**I.B. TAURIS**
LONDON • NEW YORK • OXFORD • NEW DELHI • SYDNEY

I.B. TAURIS
Bloomsbury Publishing Plc
50 Bedford Square, London, WC1B 3DP, UK
1385 Broadway, New York, NY 10018, USA
29 Earlsfort Terrace, Dublin 2, Ireland

BLOOMSBURY, I.B. TAURIS and the I.B. Tauris logo
are trademarks of Bloomsbury Publishing Plc

First published in Great Britain 2021

Copyright © Simon Cottee, 2021

Simon Cottee has asserted his right under the Copyright,
Designs and Patents Act, 1988, to be identified as Author of this work.

Cover design by Adriana Brioso
Cover image © Abstract Aerial Art/Getty Images

All rights reserved. No part of this publication may be reproduced or
transmitted in any form or by any means, electronic or mechanical, including
photocopying, recording, or any information storage or retrieval system,
without prior permission in writing from the publishers.

Bloomsbury Publishing Plc does not have any control over, or responsibility for,
any third-party websites referred to or in this book. All internet addresses given
in this book were correct at the time of going to press. The author and publisher
regret any inconvenience caused if addresses have changed or sites have
ceased to exist, but can accept no responsibility for any such changes.

A catalogue record for this book is available from the British Library.

A catalog record for this book is available from the Library of Congress.

ISBN:  HB:    978-0-7556-1693-0
       PB:    978-0-7556-1692-3
       ePDF:  978-0-7556-1695-4
       eBook: 978-0-7556-1694-7

Typeset by Integra Software Services Pvt. Ltd.

To find out more about our authors and books visit www.bloomsbury.com
and sign up for our newsletters

*To Azard Ali*

*In the same area I met up with a brother who was a sniper from the Caribbean ... I asked him about his path to guidance and how he arrived to the Islamic State. He replied, "I read about jihad in the Quran and contemplated its verses, such as the statement of Allah, 'Go forth, whether light or heavy' (At-Tawbah 41), at which point I began to search for the path to jihad. When the Islamic State was announced, my brother and I raced towards it, and Allah facilitated for us the path to reach it, and to Him belong all praise and grace." So I said to him jokingly, "We will return to the Caribbean as conquerors—with Allah's permission—and eat from your fish, and from its coconuts and bananas." At which he replied, "Never. I don't want anything except Jannah."*

*Rumiyah 12, August 6, 2017*

*These were not your average young "don't-give-a-damn" Trinidadians. These men ... were about serious business, life and death business.*
    Raoul A. Pantin, *Days of Wrath: The 1990 Coup in Trinidad and Tobago*, (Lincoln, NE: iUniverse, 2007), p. 46.

*How can yall really call this a paradise?*

*Aliya Abdul Haqq, Facebook,*
*August 15, 2014.*

# Contents

| | |
|---|---|
| Map of Trinidad and Tobago | x |
| Glossary of Islamic and Trini Terms | xi |
| | |
| Prologue: Holy War in Trinidad | 1 |
| 1  My Son the Jihadist | 7 |
| 2  The Jihad Goes Local: Yasin Abu Bakr and the 1990 Coup | 19 |
| 3  The Jihad Goes Global: ISIS and the Trini Mujahideen | 31 |
| 4  The Imam | 53 |
| 5  Homeland Insecurity | 71 |
| 6  The Lost Generation | 97 |
| Conclusion | 119 |
| | |
| Author's Note | 128 |
| Notes | 132 |
| Further Reading | 158 |
| Index | 159 |

# Map of Trinidad and Tobago

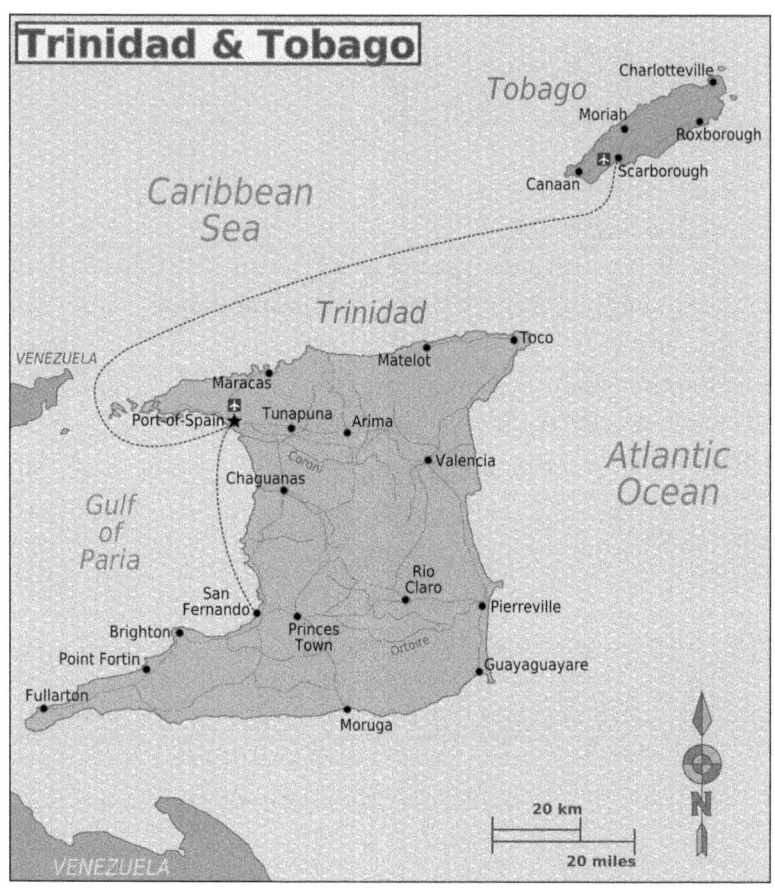

Source: Google Maps

# Glossary of Islamic and Trini Terms

| | |
|---|---|
| **abaya** | a garment of clothing for both sexes, covering most of the body |
| **alhamdulillah** | "thanks and Praise to God" |
| **aloo pie** | a fried dumpling with a spicy mashed potato filling |
| **akhi** | brother |
| **apostate** | someone who has renounced his or her faith |
| **bacchanal** | a public row, scandal, quarreling, confusion |
| **bay'ah** | an oath of allegiance to a leader |
| **bullin** | to copulate |
| **burka** | full face and body covering |
| **caliph** | a leader of Islam who claims succession from Muhammad |
| **channa** | chickpeas |
| **dawah** | the proselytizing or preaching of Islam |
| **Dawla, al-** | the state |
| **doubles** | a street-food snack made with two baras (deep fried flatbread) filled with curried chickpeas |
| **deen** | religion or belief |
| **dunya** | the temporal world |
| **emir** | leader, commander |
| **ghusl** | ritual cleansing/bath |
| **hadith** | reports relating to the sayings and deeds of the Prophet Muhammad; some collections are considered more authentic and reliable than others |
| **hajj** | the annual pilgrimage to Mecca in Saudi Arabia, which every adult Muslim of either sex must make at least once in their lifetime |
| **hijab** | covering; a veil that covers the head and chest |
| **hijrah** | migration to Islamic territory |
| **hoss** | friend |
| **imam** | leader in prayer; leader of the Muslim community |
| **iman** | faith; belief |
| **inshallah** | "if God wills" |
| **jihad** | struggle for the sake of God (including military engagement) |

| | |
|---|---|
| jannah | heaven |
| jus | just |
| kafir | an unbeliever |
| kuffar | plural of the above |
| keffiyeh | a traditional Middle Eastern headdress worn by men |
| kunya | nom de guerre |
| lime/liming | to hang out, to go drinking |
| maxi-taxis | minibuses that operate along fixed routes and are color-coded according to destination |
| mujahid | Islamic fighter |
| mujahideen | plural of the above |
| nasheeds | an Islamic song or hymn, performed without music |
| niqab | garment of clothing that covers the face, showing only eyes |
| nutting | nothing |
| Puncheon | a brand of inexpensive Trinidadian white-rum, notorious for its paint-stripping quality |
| rahmah | mercy |
| roti | a type of Indian flatbread, to be eaten alongside or filled with curried chickpeas or meats |
| sahwah | uprising, awakening |
| salafi | a term used to denote those who rigorously follow the example of the companions (*Salaf*) of the Prophet |
| sallallahu alaihi wasallam | "Praise be upon him" |
| shahid | witness/martyr |
| shalwar kameez | a long tunic worn over a pair of baggy trousers |
| soca | the national music of T&T |
| steups | an expression of annoyance or derision made by sucking air and saliva through the teeth |
| subhanallah | "glory be to God" |
| takfir | the practice of declaring another Muslim an apostate |
| taqiyyah | concealment, dissimulation |
| tawhid | oneness of God |
| ting | thing |
| Trini | Trinidadian, Trinbagonian; citizen of T&T |
| T&T | Trinidad and Tobago |
| yuh | you |

| | |
|---|---|
| **ummah** | the community or nation of Islam, composed of all Muslims worldwide |
| **umrah** | a pilgrimage to Mecca, performed by Muslims that can be undertaken at any time of the year |
| **washin dey mout** | bad talking on someone, speaking ill of another person |
| **zakat** | alms-giving, charity |
| **zina** | adultery |

# Prologue: Holy War in Trinidad

It was a gloomy and wet November morning in a busy shopping district in central Trinidad when the killer calmly walked up to the white Nissan, motionless at a red traffic-light, and opened fire. At the adjacent KFC, which was doing a brisk trade on the first Sunday of the Christmas shopping season, a few customers gathered by the window to see what was going on, but they were in no rush to go out and investigate further. The two men inside the car were killed instantly. Both were shot twice in the chest at point-blank range.[1] According to the forensic pathologist who conducted the autopsy on the victims, one was shot directly in the heart, destroying it completely, while the other sustained a bullet to the aorta.[2] The killer, whose carefully choreographed movements were captured on a CCTV camera, strolled back to the car he came in and sped off with two accomplices.

Around ten minutes later the police intercepted the car and arrested the driver. But by this point the killer and the other accomplice were gone.

Press reports in Trinidad confirmed the identity of the two victims as Joel Malchan, 29, and Dharmendra Sookdeo, 21. Malchan's brother told a journalist that he and his family had no idea why anyone would want to kill Joel. "I am baffled. I don't know if it was a jealousy thing. I don't know if it was because of the company he kept. I really don't know," he said.[3] Sookdeo's father was more forthcoming on the matter. Referring to his son, he said: "You know how many times I warned that boy about Malchan, but he wouldn't listen. Since he start *liming* [hanging out] with that boy he getting into all kinds of trouble, stealing from people. I feel sad to say this, but better he die than to be stealing from people."[4]

What press reports didn't confirm, however, was the identity of the suspected killer, although one report did reveal the name of the getaway driver, who was charged with possession of a round of ammunition and released on bail.[5]

Chaguanas, the borough in which the double murder took place, is notorious in Trinidad for crime and gang violence. In April 2018 the *T&T Express* declared it the "murder capital of T&T."[6] But this hit, carried out in November 2013, was no mere gangland killing, and these killers were not the usual pumped-up and pimped-out thugs who terrorized the neighborhood. Stuart Mohamed, the getaway driver, was from a wealthy East Indian family and worked as an IT Manager at an international packaging company owned by his parents. The triggerman—Milton Algernon—was an Afro-Trinidadian convert to Islam who had previously been arrested in 2011 on suspicion of conspiring to kill the then Prime Minister of T&T Kamla Persad-Bissessar.[7] The third accomplice in the murder—Shane Crawford—was also an Afro-Trinidadian convert to Islam and he, too, had been arrested on suspicion of involvement in the same alleged conspiracy in 2011. All three were militant Salafis who had come under the influence of Nazim Mohammed, a feared and fiery imam from the south of the country. And within weeks of the double murder all three were in Syria fighting for ISIS, the first Trinis to have done so.

When Crawford referred back to this episode in a profile interview in ISIS's now-defunct propaganda magazine *Dabiq*,[8] he said that the motive for the hit was vengeance,[9] but he didn't explain what he and his accomplices were avenging, other than referring to some "wrongs" that had been inflicted on "Muslims in the community." Whatever the motive, it was clearly a hinge-moment for the three killers: a symbolic point of no return marking their transformation into real-deal jihadis. It was also proof-positive, from the perspective of their warped worldview, that they were firm in their faith: firm enough, at any rate, to kill and die for it. "We would later look back at this moment," Crawford reflected, "and say that perhaps it was a final test from Allah to see if we were worthy of being granted the honor of hijrah [migration] and jihad."[10] In other words, if they didn't have the stomach to slaughter "*kafirs*" [unbelievers] on the streets of Chaguanas, they most definitely wouldn't have the fortitude to slaughter scores of them in a war zone in defense of the caliphate.

Two-and-a-half years after the Chaguanas double murder, Roodal Moonilal, an opposition Member of Parliament, claimed that over 400 T&T nationals had left Trinidad to join ISIS in Syria and Iraq.[11] "The government has information on the most significant security threat facing T&T and our generation—the threat of ISIS infiltrating the Caribbean and T&T," he said in parliament, theatrically holding up a thick sheaf of documents to support his claims. "What are you doing about it?," he demanded to know. It was around this time that I decided to go to Trinidad, where I had once lived and taught as a lecturer in criminology at the University of the West Indies (UWI). I wanted to find out who was going to Syria and Iraq and why. And I wanted to see those documents.

In a travelogue essay on Saint Lucia, an island north of Trinidad, the novelist Martin Amis described the place, condescendingly, as "both beautiful and innocuous, like its people."[12] "Even at its most rank and jungly," he continued, "St Lucia has a kiddybook harmlessness."[13] This is all very far from Trinidad, where away from the tourist spots at Maracas beach and the Queen's Park Oval Cricket ground, you can feel an edge on the streets, especially after dark, and where any trace of condescension will earn you a cold, hard *steups* [a sucking noise made with the tongue pressed against the teeth] and possibly worse, like getting held up at gunpoint, which happened to me within six months of arriving in the country in 2007.

On the night I returned to St. Augustine, a town in the northwest and home to UWI, there was a double murder just a block away from where I was staying. The number of murders for the year—this was 2016—was already 77, and it was still only February. This was unprecedented, even for Trinidad, where the "overall crime and safety situation" was rated by the US State Department as "critical" in 2016, with 420 murders in 2015.[14] By late June, when I made a second trip to the island, the number of murders for 2016 had soared to 227, a 15 percent increase on the 196 murders over the same period in 2015. On November 11, it reached 400.

These two trips were followed by half a dozen more. In total, between 2016 and 2018, I spent over four months in Trinidad, interviewing radical Islamists, cops, politicians, journalists, "community activists," imams, Muslims from all walks of life, and family members and friends of Trini foreign fighters.

T&T is a small twin-Island republic with a population of 1.3 million,[15] including around 104,000 Muslims.[16] Although there are comparable numbers of Muslims in neighboring Guyana and Suriname,[17] T&T is the focus of Muslim life in the Caribbean: it is home to at least eighty-five mosques and attracts a steady flow of missionaries and speakers from Saudi Arabia. It is also, less enviably, one of the world's biggest recruiting grounds of ISIS, per capita, in the world—bigger even than Belgium,[18] home to the Molenbeek jihadists who orchestrated the November 2015 Paris attacks, France's deadliest since the Second World War.

For those who assume that Trinidad is some idyllic Caribbean getaway, this will no doubt come as a shock. How could a country famed for calypso, rum and carnival produce something as monstrously obscene as fanatical Muslims intoxicated on violent religious dogma and sectarian hatred? It seems inexplicable, out of kilter, wrong. It is even a shock to Trinis, who, publicly at least, are the most energetic purveyors of the myth that Trinidad is a paradise, all the while bickering among themselves about declining moral standards, rising crime, poor schooling, endemic corruption and the price of *doubles* [a street food made of chickpeas and bread]. This myth-making is at its most brazen in the *T&T Daily Express* feature "What I love about T&T," where Trinis wax lyrical about how blessed they are to live in "sweet" T&T. "We're such a wonderful country with so many beautiful people," a certain Cindy Mohammed told the paper on June 14, 2016. "We're a melting pot of cultures and this makes us very unique. I'm very proud to be a Trini." The rest of the paper, however, is taken up with unashamedly voyeuristic stories on everything that Trinis aren't proud of: gruesome traffic accidents, political incompetence and corruption, sexual violence, domestic abuse, ferocious flooding, rising obesity rates, and the latest murder figures for the year.

As part of my day-job as a lecturer on crime and terrorism, I had closely followed the rise of ISIS in Syria and Iraq, and had written widely about it for *The Atlantic*. Like many Trinis, I was surprised that the group had found fertile soil in Trinidad, but I wasn't shocked. Having lived in Trinidad and inhaled the non-fiction of V.S. Naipaul, who is unforgiving and severe about his homeland, I knew full well that Trinidad, despite its numerous riches and delights, was not a paradise. And I knew all about the tumultuous recent political history of the country and its wrenching and bitter entanglement with Islamist zealotry. I am referring to the attempted coup in 1990, when on July 27 of that year a group of mostly black Muslims—the Jamaat al Muslimeen (JAM)—led by Yasin Abu Bakr, a convert to Islam and former police officer, stormed into the nation's Parliament in the capital city of Port of Spain and tried to overthrow the government, shooting then-Prime Minister Arthur Robinson and taking several members of his cabinet hostage.[19] The coup—the first Islamist insurrection in the West—lasted six days, after which the JAM surrendered and the government regained control. Nearly thirty years have passed since Bakr and his men launched their attack, but it still casts a long shadow over the country.

Driving from the airport into Port of Spain you cannot help but notice the rank, garbage-strewn squalor of the boiling Beetham estate, a no-go area even for Trinidad's heavily armed and heavy-handed cops. And if you drive further afield you will see deserted and decaying half-built constructions, a sign of the corruption that stalks the country like a bad *Puncheon*-fueled hangover. But Beetham and the even more notorious Laventille estate is no Molenbeek, and Trinidad, culturally and politically, is a world away from Belgium, where secularism rules and second- and third-generation Muslims have had difficulty integrating into the wider society.

Cindy Mohammed is right: Trinidad is a melting pot, and one into which most of the country's Muslims have harmoniously assimilated. Trinidad is also a highly conservative society, where tolerance, though rarely extended to gays (the country's Sexual Offences Act prohibits "buggery" and "serious indecency" between two men), is positively lavished on religious believers, and where debates over the hijab have come down firmly in favor of hijab wearers,[20] unlike in Europe where anti-Muslim bigotry is on the rise. (In T&T it was not even illegal to marry a child until the government outlawed the practice in January 2017.[21]) And despite the pockets of poverty, Trinidad is a relatively wealthy country, rich in oil and gas, where even the most feckless and workshy can carve out a half-decent life.

If there is a fault line running through Trinidadian society, which there undoubtedly is, it is the fault line of race, not religion. It is the division between black Africans, who came to the country in the 1500s as slaves and East Indians, who came much later in 1845 as indentured laborers. The East Indians are vastly wealthier than the blacks, who unsurprisingly resent the disparity. This division is also reflected in the Muslim *ummah* [community] in Trinidad, where the mainstream Islamic organizations are made up largely of East Indians, and where the more fundamentalist groups, like the JAM, draw on a largely black membership and feel marginalized from the Indo-Trini Muslim mainstream.

How, then, was a nascent, self-proclaimed Islamic State, situated around 10,000 kilometers from a prosperous, multi-racial democratic country at the southernmost point of the Caribbean archipelago, able to capture the hearts and minds of a small number of citizens from that country and from across its racial divide, prompting them to desert it for a new life in a strange land riven by war? This book tries to answer that question, and in doing so sheds a light on why men and women who live a world away from the sectarian conflicts of the Middle East would choose to risk everything and sacrifice their own relative comforts and certainties for a chance to join a violent cause in a place whose history, customs, and language couldn't be more different from their own.

# 1

# My Son the Jihadist

*11 months ago, 29-year-old Shane Crawford sold his valuables—a van and a big screen TV—to make up money for the airfare to go to war-torn Syria.*
Mark Fraser, "Why My Son Fights with ISIS,"<br>T&T Daily Express, October 10, 2014

*I woulda put my head on a block that no Trini gunman would be in that [ISIS] ... but they may live longer fighting in Syria than living in Enterprise and they know that.*
Post by VII, Topic Thread: "Chaguanas/Enterprise War Zone,"<br>http://trinituner.com, March 30, 2017, 12:00 a.m.

In the summer of 2016, when ISIS still controlled large areas of territory in Syria and Iraq, the group published what was to be the last installment of its online magazine *Dabiq*. Entitled "Break the Cross," it was full of violent condemnations and warnings against multiple enemies, with a particular focus on "pagan Christians." It also contained, in what had become a standard feature, an interview with an ISIS foreign fighter. "When I was around twenty years old I would come to accept the religion of truth, Islam," said Abu Sa'd at-Trinidadi, recalling how he had turned away from the Christian faith he was born into.[1] At-Trinidadi, as his *kunya* [nom de guerre] suggests, was from T&T. Asked if he had a message for "the Muslims of Trinidad," he castigated his co-religionists at home for remaining in "a place where you have no honor and are forced to live in humiliation, subjugated by the disbelievers."[2]

This message was aimed not just at T&T's East Indian Muslim population, who make up the majority of Muslims in the country, but also at Afro-Trinidadian Muslim converts, particularly those associated with the Jamaat al Muslimeen (JAM), a fringe group which tried to overthrow the government of T&T in July 1990.[3] Chillingly, at-Trinidadi urged Muslims in T&T to wage jihad against their fellow citizens: "Terrify the disbelievers in their own homes and make their streets run with their blood."[4]

Abu Sa'd at-Trinidadi's real name was Shane Crawford. Before the interview with *Dabiq* only a few Trinis had heard of him, but after it he became a badge of national shame in Trinidad. It had also put a giant target on his head, and within weeks of its publication he was severely injured in a US drone strike. He never recovered and died from his wounds in February 2017. About a month later, at the end of March, and despite his demise,[5] the US State Department added him to its list of "Specially Designated Global Terrorists."[6]

Crawford is not the first Trini to have made his way on to such a list. In 2015 the T&T High Court designated Kareem Ibrahim a terrorist. Ibrahim, who is now dead, was convicted in the United States and sentenced to life imprisonment in 2012 for plotting to blow up the John F. Kennedy (JFK) Airport in New York in 2007.[7] But no other Trini—with the possible exception of the disgraced former FIFA vice-president Jack Warner—has matched Crawford's global notoriety.

Who is Shane Crawford and how did he become a "Global Terrorist"?

In search of answers, I paid a visit to the neighborhood where Crawford grew up, Enterprise, and where his mother Joan still lives. A friend, a cop who grew up in the JAM, told me not to go there, on account that I might get robbed or kidnapped or caught up in the crossfire between "Unruly ISIS" and Rasta City, the two gangs that operate in the town. But the only menace I encountered was the sound of a hiss, which may or may not have been directed at me. In any case, I didn't hang around, for there wasn't much to see. Enterprise is just like any other town in Trinidad: all concrete and corrugated iron and burglar bars, humming to the beat of *soca* or reggae music thundering from blacked-out car windows, rum shops, and *roti* joints. As I walked past a carwash I saw a man sleeping on the sidewalk. A few brothers were idling around nearby, smoking cigarettes the size of Christmas trees. The traffic was busy, as it always is in Trinidad, but there didn't seem to be much enterprise going on in Enterprise when I was there.

A ten-minute *Maxi* ride away is the Al Khaleefah mosque in Longdenville, where Crawford would often pray.[8] The mosque's imam, Lennox Agard, a thick-set former reggae artist who went by the name of Edoo Rankin, was detained in February 2018 in relation to an alleged terrorist plot targeting the annual Carnival celebrations.[9]

The house where Shane grew up and where Joan lives is modest, even by Trinidad's standards. Joan told me, in a tone of hurt and incredulity, how a local journalist who had interviewed her about Shane had described the place as "dilapidated," which is ungenerous and rude, if not wholly inaccurate. Joan is obviously a very proud woman and nowhere is her pride more in evidence, and more on the line, than when she talks about her beloved Shane.

The interview did not start well. When Joan, who was dressed in a green *abaya* and tightly fitted black hijab, opened the door to me, I extended my hand to her, but she declined to shake it. "We don't do that," she politely said, with a heavy hint of self-righteousness. I should have known better. I should have also known not to have worn effeminate cotton ankle socks, which Joan surveyed with a flash of distaste when I removed my shoes. But as we spoke she started to warm to me. I told her I wanted to understand who the "real" Shane was and what made him tick. I told her I wanted to understand what it was like to live with the stigma of having a son join ISIS. And it was true, but I also wanted to know how Shane had got to Syria and what he did when he was there. I wanted to know about his criminal past, and who he had associated with in Trinidad. And I wanted to know just how serious he was in his faith and how he reconciled his criminal badass self with his faith-based one.

"My son was never recruited by anyone in this country," Joan told me as soon as I started recording the interview, deviating from the standard script reeled off by the parents of jihadists, who find solace in the belief that their son or daughter was "brainwashed" by shadowy recruiters—and thus not fully responsible for their actions.

> He was following the news, everything that was going on in the world, with the Muslims, and then I think what really triggered it off was that he saw that some sisters left somewhere from Africa and went to Syria to help their Muslim sisters, because they were being raped and killed and *ting*. So he say, 'Why were these women leave and go to give support to their sisters, and what am I doing as a man, what am I doing as a Muslim?' And that is when my son decided to leave, you know. There was never a recruiter. And after my son left with two of his friends the word started to spread. And then when the media put it out, that's when Trinis started leaving. So the media, really, was the person that was recruiting here.

Shane left Trinidad with his wife, a woman named Jamelia Luqman, at the end of November in 2013—just days after the double murder in Chaguanas. But it wasn't until nine months later that his leaving became public knowledge in Trinidad, when a video was posted on YouTube of Shane, Milton Algernon, and another man jumping into the Euphrates River in Syria. As Shane prepares to address the camera, one of the men off camera tells him, "*Akhi* [brother], your ass is showing man," which makes Shane crack up laughing. He then triumphantly declares, "I jus made *ghusl* [ritual cleansing]. In the Euphrates. In Minus one degrees!" This is the "banal" face of evil that the German-American political theorist Hannah Arendt wrote about,[10] killers unmasked, resembling more frat boys than murderous zealots. Not that Joan would ever accept that Shane was capable of evil, banal or otherwise.

In another video that surfaced around the same time, first posted on Liveleak, a video-sharing website that trades in graphic gore porn, an ISIS militant is shown holding up a severed head.[11] "Hello, my name is John," he says in a mock English accent, performing the role of ventriloquist. "Right now John look like he died of natural causes," a voice says off-camera. It bears a striking resemblance to Shane's voice, but this has never been verified.

Shane was the last of Joan's six children, but clearly first in her affections. "I could not have deserved a better child," Joan said. "From a baby, I never had problems. No problems at all. He used to call me mommy dearest." She recalled that when she fell ill in 2005 and was admitted to hospital for six weeks Shane was the ever-dutiful son, bringing her food that he had cooked at home. At this point in the interview Joan started to break down. The wound of losing him was still clearly raw for her, especially so in remembering how tender and loving Shane could be with her.

As a teenager growing up in Enterprise, there was always a danger that Shane would fall into bad company. But he was a homebody, and spent most of his time indoors watching movies and playing video games. It was around this time that Joan was working as a nurse in New York and Shane was living with his stepfather back in Trinidad. He was a bright kid, she said, proudly handing me an album of his various diplomas and certificates.

He was born and raised as a Christian Baptist, as was Joan. But he converted out of the faith and became a Muslim when he was 20. "My son did take his Islam seriously," Joan said. "When he revert to Islam he had a girlfriend, and he told her, 'We cannot be friends anymore.'" They later married, but only after she had become a Muslim. Joan, too, converted to Islam, although she was reticent about how this self-transformation happened and what role, if any, Shane played in it.

Though bright, Shane was not an exceptional student, and was always between jobs after he graduated from college. He found work as a laborer and when that fell through he did a stint as a cab driver. For his last job he sold fish along the Southern Main Road in Enterprise.

Like many young hardcore Western Salafis, Shane cuts a contradictory figure. According to Joan, he loved American mafia movies, which he would watch on his big flat-screen TV, but he hated America for its materialism and war-making in the Middle East. He didn't mind war-making on the "*kuffars*" in Enterprise, however. One acquaintance of Shane's told the *T&T Daily Express*: "He was a man who would take his Muslim wear seriously. He was always wearing his clothes. Even when he was selling fish ... But he was also a ladies man, he always had these girls around him."[12] Barrington "Skippy" Thomas, a political activist and radio talk-show host, described Shane, who he knew for many years and helped fund his move into the fishing business, as "an idealist, a disciplinarian—hated weed, coke and crime." "He was against injustice and oppression—an angry young man," he told the *T&T Guardian*, adding that when he saw him three days before he left for Syria, "He said he intended to 'participate in an exercise that would transform T&T from a swamp of injustice to an oasis of justice.'"[13] Shane didn't tell Thomas where he was heading, and Thomas apparently didn't ask.

As Joan tells it, things started to go bad for Shane in 2011, when in September of that year he was charged with possession of a Glock pistol, 110 rounds of ammunition, four firearm magazines, an army uniform, and a bullet-proof vest. He was jointly charged with his wife Jamelia Luqman, then 22 and a university student, and Milton Algernon.[14] Two months later, while out on bail and not long after the T&T government had declared a state of emergency [SOE], he was arrested again, with fifteen others, on suspicion of plotting to assassinate Prime Minister Kamla Persad-Bissessar and senior members of her cabinet. Despite being detained for fourteen days he was not charged. None of the sixteen men were, due to lack of sufficient evidence.[15]

Joan thinks that this radicalized Shane. "You know how difficult it is for him to get a work after his own country branded him a terrorist? Wanting to kill his own Prime Minister? It affected him," she told the *T&T Daily Express* in 2014.[16] Three years earlier, in the same paper, Shane relayed just how much he had been bruised by the experience, viewing it as part of a broader religious persecution against Muslims:

> It hurt me to see that this is a country of democracy where everybody has equal rights and it was only Muslims that were scraped together, some of them didn't even know each other, and implicated as the people who were trying to destabilise the country ... My name has been tarnished to the point that I cannot work nor do business because once I produce my name anywhere it's going to raise eyebrows and people are going to look at me differently, even though I am innocent

of everything the government and the police have labelled against me. I am traumatised by what has happened, my wife and son have been affected and I am still trying to figure how I am going to provide for my family.[17]

In *Dabiq*, Shane alluded to this episode, absent the above tone of anguished self-pity: "That would have been an honor for us to attempt, but the reality of our operations was much smaller," he told the ISIS magazine, referring to the alleged plot to kill Persad-Bissessar.[18] In the same interview, he had also spoken scathingly of the "religion of democracy," which stands in stark contrast with the wounded disappointment he expressed in the *T&T Daily Express* about how T&T had failed to live up to its democratic promise to treat all its citizens equally.

Marc Sageman, a forensic psychiatrist and former CIA case officer, has suggested that the defining moment in the radicalization process occurs when personal discontent becomes entangled with public grievance, so that it takes on a wider political significance and becomes weaponized as a collective harm that must be avenged.[19] Perhaps one reason why Shane found militant Salafism so appealing was because it resonated with, and helped rationalize, his own personal sense of victimization—or rather his own persecution-complex. Perhaps another was that it gave him a ready-made justification for violence and lawlessness: a way of violently exorcizing his inner demons. When Shane, in *Dabiq*, spoke of Trinidad as a place where Muslims "have no honor and are forced to live in humiliation,"[20] few of his co-religionists would have recognized this as a remotely fair or accurate portrayal of their country, but it seems to be indicative of how Shane himself felt: more sinned against than sinning, a noble victim of an evil conspiracy. He could pretend that all his failures and problems had nothing to do with his own ill-conceived actions or personal limitations or character flaws, but were entirely the fault of other culprits in Trinidad who sought to persecute him solely because he was a Muslim. It was, of course, a demented fiction, but it was a highly serviceable one for Shane.

Strikingly, of the sixteen all-Muslim suspects arrested on suspicion of plotting to kill the Prime Minister, four ended up in Syria and Iraq: Shane, Algernon, Ashmead Choate, and Zaid Abdul Hamid. All four men knew each other. In *Dabiq*, Shane singled out Choate for particular praise:

> By Allah's grace, there was a man of sound knowledge who I was able to refer to and who would answer any questions I had. His name was Shaykh Ashmead Choate and he had studied *hadith* and graduated from one of the Islamic colleges in the Middle East. He made hijrah [migration] to the Islamic State and attained martyrdom fighting in Ramadi.[21]

Choate, a former principal of an Islamic school in Freeport, which is a ten-minute drive from Chaguanas and where Shane's wife Jamila also worked as a teacher, was in his late fifties when he traveled to Iraq in 2015, where he lasted about six months.

According to Joan, Shane was motivated more by humanitarian concern than religious zeal. "They are killing my Muslim sisters, raping them, killing the children, and I am here to help," he reportedly told her in a Skype conversation a week after he had arrived in Syria. Joan also believes that Shane was searching for a greater purpose in life and that in ISIS and Syria he had found it. Yet it is hard to reconcile this secularized and sanitized image of Shane with the one brashly on show in *Dabiq*, where he comes across as a violent religious extremist. Here he regrets that in T&T there are very few Muslims "upon the sound creed."[22] Indeed, he castigates them as "apostates having nothing to do with Islam except its name."[23] Addressing those who "have neglected to perform hijrah [migration]," he urges them to find redemption by attacking "the interests of the Crusader coalition near you, including their embassies, businesses, and 'civilians'. Burn down their government institutions just as they try to bomb our buildings where Allah's law is upheld. Follow the example of the lions in France and Belgium, the example of the blessed couple in California, and the examples of the knights in Orlando and Nice."[24] He confides that his greatest goal in life was to "join the mujahidin striving to cleanse the Muslims' usurped lands of all apostate regimes."[25] And he confessed to the double murder in Chaguanas in 2013:

> **Dabiq:** After making the decision to perform hijrah to the Levant [Syria] with two of your closest friends, Abu 'Abdillah [Milton Algernon] and Abu 'Isa [Stuart Mohamed], you experienced some delay. What happened?
>
> **Abu Sa'd at-Trinidadi [Shane]:** The three of us decided to make hijrah to the Levant and join the Islamic State after witnessing the plight of the Muslims in the Levant, but [before leaving] we had some unfinished business with some disbelievers who had wronged the Muslims in the community ... The operation was carried out in the middle of the city in broad day light and was caught on camera. It wasn't our plan for it to occur that way, but it happened according to Allah's decree. Following the operation, Abu 'Abdillah [Algernon] and Abu 'Isa [Mohamed] were arrested, and I went into hiding. We decided that we had to leave Trinidad nonetheless because nothing was going to stop our hijrah, by Allah's permission. Once more, Allah bestowed a tremendous favor on us as Abu 'Isa was released pending investigation. Abu 'Abdillah was also released and we left Trinidad one-by-one. I left first along with my wife, followed by Abu 'Abdillah, and then Abu 'Isa, and we met up in Venezuela.[26]

When I asked Joan about Shane's involvement in the murder and all his blood-curdling rhetoric in *Dabiq*, she dodged the question. "I am not the judge. Only god is the judge." Yet she had plenty of negative judgments to make about US imperialism and what she saw as its ill-effects on Trinidad, particularly Trini womanhood. "Women these days don't value themselves," she said, lamenting that the pornification of American culture had reached Trinidad.

Most parents of those who have joined ISIS deny that they knew anything about their plans to leave. Did Joan know that Shane was going? She said he left without telling her, recalling that the first time she heard was during a Skype conversation: He said, "Mom, I'm in Syria, what you crying for?" "I will never see you again," Joan told him. "Not in this life, but we will meet in *Jannah* [heaven], *inshallah* ['if God wills']," replied Shane.

Most parents of ISIS devotees are also keen to distance themselves from their son's or daughter's decision to join ISIS by either condemning ISIS or insisting that their children were tricked or indoctrinated into joining the group. Not Joan. Clearly Shane's departure upset her. But it doesn't seem to have disturbed her, morally speaking. She wasn't even ambivalent about it. Quite the opposite: "He always a leader, stuck in his ways. He died for what he believed in and how many of us are willing to do that?"

Other Trini parents of ISIS members have expressed the same sentiment, the same barefaced, bloody-minded defense of their son's or daughter's decision to give their lives to a genocidal terrorist group which the vast majority of Muslims outside of T&T have violently condemned. When the *T&T Newsday* interviewed the father of Mikail Ali, a 27-year-old who was killed in an airstrike in Syria in August 2016, he said: "This is happiness. We know where he has gone. We are happy. Only a Muslim will understand that … We all have to die."[27] He then added, almost menacingly: "How do you defeat an enemy who looks into the barrel of a gun and sees paradise?"

The father of 23-year-old Fahyim Sabur, who died on the battlefield in Syria, was similarly unabashed in his comments to a journalist about his son's death: "I felt elated. Speaking about it now, I am overelated." Fahyim, like Shane, was also from Enterprise, where he gave private Arabic lessons in the neighborhood.[28]

Although Shane's *Dabiq* interview sheds an interesting light on his life before he reached the caliphate, it is vague on his life inside it. He says that he was a sniper, and he mentions that Algernon, Mohamed, and Choate all died as martyrs in different battles, but he doesn't say much else, obviously not wanting to compromise his security.

Joan, too, was evasive about what Shane had done in Syria, but she did say that he fathered another two children when he was there with his wife Jamila, and that when Algernon was killed, Shane married his widow, becoming the father to his five children in Syria. Joan also told me that she thought Shane was a commander in ISIS, or at any rate "high up," and that he would always call her from an office, where he looked all business. She was clearly impressed by this, and while most parents of ISIS foreign fighters are content to believe that their son was far from the frontline, performing the non-violent duties of, say, a cook or a mechanic, Joan's pride in knowing that Shane was in the thick of it is barely concealed.

In October 2016, just two months after Shane's *Dabiq* interview was published, he was seriously injured in a US drone strike on a convoy of cars he was in. When Joan first heard the news it was via a WhatsApp message from one of Shane's friends in Syria. Shane died of his injuries a few months later in February 2017. At the end of March of that same year Faris Al-Rawi, the attorney general, obtained an injunction from the High Court of T&T declaring Shane a listed terrorist entity and ordering the seizure of his assets in accordance with the provisions of the country's Anti-Terrorism Act.[29] It was a quintessentially Trini gesture: all talk and all too late. And, in any case, as Joan told me, Shane had already sold his most prized possessions—a big TV and a van—before he went to Syria.

Of all the many things that Shane says in his *Dabiq* interview, one of the most telling is his reference to the 1990 attempted coup, when he would have been just 5 years old:

> There was a faction of Muslims in Trinidad that was known for 'militancy.' Its members attempted to overthrow the disbelieving government but quickly surrendered, apostatized, and participated in the religion of democracy, demonstrating that they weren't upon the correct methodology of jihad.[30]

The faction of Muslims Shane is referring to is the Jamaat al Muslimeen (JAM). In Trinidad and beyond, the JAM is widely considered to be an extremist organization, yet here is Shane, courtesy of those sardonic inverted commas around the word militancy, pouring scorn on its radical credentials, and castigating it for collusion in the democratic politics of T&T. Indeed, here is Shane declaring Yasin Abu Bakr and his men "apostates" no less—traitors to the faith. And everyone knows what the punishment for apostasy in Islam is: death.[31]

It is thus ironic that when the world's news media started coming to Trinidad in 2017 to report on ISIS recruitment there the first person they visited in search of answers was Yasin Abu Bakr, the semi-charismatic leader of the JAM. Now an old man and out of touch, he had little of interest to say, just the same old ramblings about the ravaging evils of oppression and poverty. No one thought to ask him about his own role in this, or about the considerable wealth and real estate he has amassed since the coup, and no one interviewed him in his well-appointed house in Diego Martin. Instead they visited him in his stark and austere compound on the outskirts of Port of Spain, as did I when I interviewed his son and heir-apparent Fuad.

Yet without Yasin Abu Bakr and the JAM there would be no Shane Crawford the "Global Terrorist." There would be no Abu Sa'd at-Trinidadi. There would be no Trini ISIS mujahideen. Because it was in Bakr's compound that the spark of jihad was first lit in Trinidad and the country would never be the same again.

2

# The Jihad Goes Local: Yasin Abu Bakr and the 1990 Coup

*A Muslim coup in a former British colonial Caribbean territory whose population, about evenly split between descendants of African slaves and Indian indentured labourers—a Muslim coup in a largely Christian and Hindu country—what did it mean?*
Pantin, Days of Wrath, p. 114

*The people of Trinidad and Tobago owe me an apology. I don't owe them any apology and I'll never apologise; they owe me an apology.*
Yasin Abu Bakr, Quoted in<br>"Jamaat boss on 1990 coup," Wired868, July 27, 2015

"He's a truly spiritual person," Fuad Abu Bakr told me, referring to his father, Yasin, the 78-year-old leader of the Jamaat al Muslimeen (JAM). We were standing in front of the mosque his father built at #1 Murcarapo Road, and at the exact spot on which this ever so spiritual soul had, on July 27, 1990, gathered his men—who were armed to the teeth with AK47s, pump-action shotguns, and rifles—for a group prayer and pep-talk just before launching an insurrection against the T&T state. According to Fuad, Yasin was seeking guidance from God, a sign that he was on the right path: "He was saying to God, 'if I'm gonna do the wrong thing, then stop me from leaving here.'" But no divine intervention was forthcoming, and Bakr and his men sped off into Port of Spain, with one group headed for the nation's Parliament in the Red House, and another to T&T's only TV station TTT (T&T Television). It was around 5:30 p.m., and it was a Friday: peak *lime*.

But this was peak jihad, and as Bakr and his men, all 114 of them, stormed into both buildings they shouted "allahu akbar!"[1] Minutes before they had shot to death a lone policeman and exploded a car bomb outside the police headquarters nearby, engulfing it in flames.[2] There was soon to be more bloodshed: within hours of laying siege to the parliament, which was still in session when the JAM stormed it, a militant had shot Prime Minister Arthur Robinson in the leg. This was punishment for a show of defiance on Robinson's part, when, ordered with a gun to his head by a JAM member to call off the approaching security forces over a radiophone, he shouted, "Murderers! Torturers! Attack with full force."[3] A female clerk was killed: this was bad luck; she was struck by one of the bullets the militants were wildly spraying around as they entered the parliament chamber.[4] Leo des Vignes, a government MP, was shot in the leg: he died from blood loss a couple of days later.[5] Other government ministers were tied up, slapped around, and roughed up. Robinson, already wounded, was made to lie on the floor with his pants pulled down.

In the TTT building, located on the outskirts of the capital and where twenty-seven hostages were being held, including Raoul Pantin, a local journalist who went on to write a brilliantly perceptive personal account of the coup (*Days of Wrath*), Bakr was preparing to address the nation. Like the stars of the present-day global jihad, Bakr instinctively understood the power of the media, as a tool both for projecting power and for stirring up sympathy.[6] Ahead of his time, Bakr knew that the jihad had to be televised. And so it was. At just after 7 p.m., TTT went on air with the most dramatic newscast in its 28-year-old history (TTT was established in the year that T&T won its independence from the British in August 1962).[7] "At 6PM this afternoon, the government of Trinidad and Tobago was overthrown," Bakr coolly told the nation. "The prime minister and members of the cabinet are under arrest. We are asking everybody to remain calm. The revolutionary forces are commanded to control the streets. There shall be no looting."[8] He then went on to declare that the army was on the side of the JAM, which was a blatant lie.[9] And he railed against Prime Minister Robinson's plans to build a statue in honor of Gene Miles, a former public servant who had campaigned against corruption in the People's National Movement (PNM) government of the late Dr. Eric Williams.[10] (Robinson was leader of the National Alliance for Reconstruction (NAR) party.) This is Bakr:

> Amidst all the poverty and destitution, where people can't find jobs, where there is no work, where children are reduced to crime in order to live, where there are no drugs in the hospitals, the Prime Minister this week, the last Prime Minister, the ex-Prime Minister, broke the camel's back when he said that half a million dollars was going to be allocated for a stone monument for Gene Miles. We could no longer take that kind of action from leaders. This is the last straw. I personally would break down that monument if it was built.[11]

It was an odd rant. Bakr, the self-declared leader of "the revolutionary forces," had just launched an armed insurrection and appeared on television to announce it, and here he was banging on about the injustice of erecting a monument in honor of a relative non-entity named Gene Miles. Yet it was deeply revealing of his mindset. For Bakr, the decision to erect the monument typified the contradictions of an unequal society that saw it fit to lavish money on an inanimate object while many thousands languished in poverty. And it typified, in his mind, the rank corruption and moral depravity of a society that saw it fit to honor, in the words of one of Bakr's lieutenants, "a social prostitute."[12] This was a reference to what Pantin euphemistically referred to as Miles's "flamboyant" lifestyle: she was a lush and was probably best known in Trinidad for her ill-fated affair with a PNM government minister and for her subsequent short-lived career as a calypso artist following her ostracism from the PNM.[13] Drawing his announcement to a close, Bakr said that he and his men had "made a noble act on your [the nation's] behalf"[14] and promised to return with further televised updates.

Despite his insistence that "there shall be no looting," there was looting—and it devastated the capital city.[15] But there was no uprising—and it devastated the coup attempt. This was the gamble the

JAM leadership had made: that once they took over the parliament and TTT, a groundswell of popular support would propel them forward to a real and durable political takeover. But it didn't happen, because while many Trinis were in sympathy with Bakr's critique of political corruption and social injustice they were not supportive of his violent contempt for democracy, much less his Islamized vision of what a fully just society should look like.[16] "We expected the people to take some kind of action," Kwesi Atiba, a JAM leader, told the social scientist Selwyn Ryan. "Some did and some didn't."[17] Or rather: some looted, and most were appalled by the JAM's violent method of conflict resolution. This included the vast majority of T&T's mostly East Indian Muslim population, who were suspicious of Bakr's group,[18] and who probably looked dimly on Bakr's inflammatory suggestion, voiced to the *T&T Sunday Express* in 1985, that they were not "really practising the true tenets of the religion."[19]

True to his word, Bakr reappeared on TV with a further update at 10:30 p.m., the nightly newscast time. Bakr, who had nothing but disdain for the rule of law, was positively obsequious in his adherence to the TTT news schedule. "Tell them," he instructed TTT news presenter Dominic Kallipersad, "that I'm the Leader of the Revolution."[20] "Mr Bakr, ah, says he's the leader of the revolution," said Kallipersad, which clearly annoyed the Leader of the Revolution, who now decided to go off script, relaying a long and boring story about the recent death of a soldier, seemingly in an effort to win some sympathy from the army, who were preparing to unleash an ungodly amount of firepower at TTT and the Red House.[21] Bakr said the government had refused the JAM's offer of free drugs and other medical supplies, which they had obtained from patrons in the Middle East, and that those drugs—which were imported through UNICEF and said to be valued at TT $800,000[22]—could have saved the life of the soldier who had died of leukemia.[23] Presumably, in Bakr's delusional mind, the government was also responsible for the death of the police officer outside the Red House earlier that very evening, but he was sensible to avoid this topic.

Bakr then announced, in a cynical attempt to solicit support from a populace that had thus far refused to join the JAM uprising, that he was abolishing VAT, the 15 percent value added sales tax that Robinson's NAR government had introduced as one of its new revenue-raising measures.[24] This was a deeply unpopular policy at a time when the country was going through a severe recession, due to a downturn in global oil prices in the early 1980s and the depletion of foreign currency reserves.

And, finally, Bakr called for the formation of a caretaker government and promised that a new general election would be held in ninety days.[25]

This was to be Bakr's last appearance as a TV news anchor in the whole six days and five nights of the coup: in the small hours of Saturday morning, the army took TTT off the air. This enraged Bakr, who, Pantin recalled, "kept insisting: 'They must put the TV station back on air! 'They must put the TV station back on air!'"[26]

In an observation that cuts to the very psychological core of Bakr, a shameless narcissist who claimed that God wanted him to overthrow the T&T government, Pantin reflected:

> It is inconceivable, though not wholly implausible, that Bakr had staged a bloody coup merely to appear on television and harangue the nation. Clearly, he enjoyed it. In his two earlier appearances on TTT that Friday night, Bakr had been the star of his own show, relishing every moment of it, switching from the angry Leader of the Revolution, to the humble Imam who was merely carrying out "the will of Allah."[27]

There is clearly something to this: Bakr courted controversy and relished the hot glare of publicity. He needed to be seen and heard, as if his life depended on it, and it's likely that had he not been able to appear on TV announcing his "heroic" takeover he may have thought twice about launching the whole undertaking. As Selwyn Ryan put it, Bakr, in almost everything he said or did, "always seemed to be trying to play to an audience, to project himself and his men as heroes."[28] But the main reason for the insurrection had little to do with Bakr's desire to be seen and heard; its root, rather, was in his acute sense of humiliation, anger, and existential threat over the state occupation of #1 Murcarapo Road. It had to do with a convoluted and ongoing land dispute. This was the life and death issue that had mobilized the JAM: not Islam, not corruption, not injustice, but real estate.[29]

The land at #1 Murcarapo Road had originally been offered to the Islamic Missionary Guild (IMG) in 1969 by the PNM government of Dr. Eric Williams.[30] The IMG had planned to use it to build an Islamic Cultural Center. But the 8 acres of mostly swampland wasn't suitable for their needs, so they sought another site. When they left, a small group of black Muslims remained, with the consent of the IMG. Under the leadership of Bakr, this group, which became the JAM, drained the land and started building on it, putting up a mosque, housing quarters, and a school. But they did so without the approval of the local government, and on land that they had no legal right to.[31] And so began the JAM's conflict with the T&T state, a dispute that stretched over three government administrations from 1983 to its bloody climax in 1990.[32]

Three episodes leading up to that climax were defining and propulsive. The first was the killing, in 1985, of JAM member Abdul Kareem while he was being escorted by the police to a police station in St James, a bustling district of Port of Spain.[33] No one was convicted of this crime and his killer or killers went unpunished. This caused tensions to spiral between the police and the JAM.

The second was the humiliation of the police inside Bakr's compound when they tried to arrest him for ignoring a court order to stop new constructions on the land at #1 Murcarapo Road. When the police arrived at the compound, Bakr had surrounded himself with women and children, resulting in the police turning back for fear of injuring the innocent bystanders that Bakr had deployed as a human shield.[34] This didn't reflect well on Bakr, for obvious reasons. But it was a public relations disaster for the police, who looked weak for backing down, and gave them an additional *casus belli* for striking against the JAM.

But by far the most combustible moment in the conflict was the occupation of the Murcarapo premises in April 1990 by the army and police. According to acting assistant commissioner of police, Dennis

Taylor, who was in charge of the occupation, the reason behind it was to "prevent the Jamaat from continuing construction without permission."[35] It probably didn't help matters that the occupation coincided with the holy month of Ramadan.

Bakr not only saw the occupation as an intolerable challenge to his moral authority; he also read it as an existential threat, believing that it was only a matter of time before the police and army would turn their weapons on him and his followers in an effort to physically destroy the JAM.[36] Two months before the insurrection, Bakr protested: "The real reason behind the invasion of the Jamaat was not to stop the building of the school, but to set the Police and Army at our throats."[37] Bakr, as he saw it, was pushed into a corner and had no choice: the only way to save the JAM from destruction was to overthrow the government. When asked, in 1993, by the criminologist Ramesh Deosaran what "really sparked" the 1990 insurrection, Bakr said: "The military occupation of April 21, 1990 ... it was a military solution to a military problem and action."[38]

Seen from this perspective, the attempted coup had nothing to do with trying to establish an Islamic state in T&T, and although Bakr and his men had professed a desire to die as martyrs—"We are going to Paradise," Pantin remembered Bakr saying on day two of the siege[39]—and proclaimed that they were selflessly acting according to the will of Allah, this was all essentially bullshit and bluster.[40] Bakr and his men, though bravely risking their lives in trying to take down the government, clearly did not want to die, and did everything in their power to avoid that outcome. What Bakr really wanted was to bring about a change in the political leadership of T&T and to usher in a new government that would accede to his claim to authority over the land at Murcarapo Road.[41]

And he and his followers were broadly successful in this: the insurrection did bring about a change in the government, and to this day Bakr maintains ownership over #1 Murcarapo Road.[42] As an unapologetic Bakr told Deosaran, "It was a military action and the action was to change the government and we succeeded in changing the government. The government is no longer there: Robinson is no longer there."[43] On December 16, 1991—seventeen months after the attempted coup—the NAR government was defeated by the PNM.

Even more gallingly for the state and country, the JAM militants were given a pardon. The basis for this had been negotiated early on in the insurrection, when it had become painfully clear to the JAM that the people of T&T had not taken to the streets in support of their rebellion. The euphoria of the first twenty-four hours had passed, and now, tired and hungry, the reality of the situation had hit Bakr and his men: they were boxed in, and had no chance of out-gunning the 1,000 man-strong T&T army outside the TTT building and the Red House. Now that the prospect of "martyrdom" was all too real, it seemed to have lost its radiant allure. So there would be no more talk about becoming *"shahids"* [martyrs] and going to paradise. Instead, Bakr was desperately trying to hammer out a deal with the "kuffar" government, whereby in return for freeing the hostages he and his men would be given a presidential pardon and full entitlement to the land at #1 Murcarapo Road. On day six of the insurrection, satisfied that they had a deal, the JAM surrendered, ceremoniously laying down their weapons as they emerged from the TTT building and the Red House. They were then detained and charged with treason and sedition. But the charges didn't stick and they were released in 1992 after their claim of amnesty was upheld.[44] It was an extraordinary end to an extraordinary episode in the history of T&T. Not only had the JAM violently attacked a democratic government, bringing chaos and confusion to the country, and causing millions of [TT] dollars in property damage, to say nothing of the physical and psychological wounds the group inflicted on their hostages; they had done all that, and then they walked, serving just two years for their treasonous crimes.

Two other things, equally extraordinary, then happened within fifteen years of the JAM's release. First, in 1999, the Port of Spain City Corporation, which owned the lands at #1 Murcarapo Road, signed a ninety-year lease with Bakr for the JAM to remain on the site. And second, in 2003, Bakr was awarded TT $2.5 million [approx.

US $350,000] by the courts for the damage done to his compound by the army on the night of July 27, 1990. The court also held Bakr liable for TT $32 million for damages the JAM caused to state property, including the destruction of the Police headquarters, during the insurrection.[45]

In July 2010—justice, like a lot of things in T&T, moves at a snail's pace—the then Attorney General of T&T, Anand Ramlogan, announced that eleven properties belonging to Bakr and another senior JAM member, estimated at over TT $9 million, were to be put up for public auction. Bakr, as ever playing the victim, described the state's civil lawsuit against him as "political persecution," complaining that "millions of dollars in debt have been written off for other people."[46]

The auction, which was held a month after Ramlogan's announcement, was not well attended, but it was crawling with JAM members, including one of Bakr's sons and one of his four wives, who successfully bid for two properties, both worth over TT $1 million.[47] Many Trinis were outraged by this outcome, while quite a few were impressed by Bakr's barefaced audacity.

Shortly after his release from prison in 1992, Bakr told a journalist, "The Muslimeen had sacrificed themselves for the poor and oppressed and would find the gates of Paradise open ... The Muslimeen had freed a colonized people, slaves, from the NAR government."[48] Bakr, in other words, was still full of it. And in the next twenty-five years drama would continue to swamp him like a cheap *shalwar kameez*. In 2003 he was charged with conspiracy to murder former JAM members Zaki Aubaida and Salim Rasheed.[49] In 2005 he was charged for sedition based on a sermon he gave in his mosque warning that "blood will flow" if wealthy Trini Muslims didn't pay *zakat* [charity] to the JAM.[50] In 2007 he came under the radar of the FBI, who suspected him of involvement in a plot to blow up fuel depots at New York's JFK International Airport. One of the co-conspirators in the plot, Kareem Ibrahim, had spent time at Bakr's mosque;[51] Ibrahim, who died in 2016, was sentenced to life imprisonment in 2012.[52] And in 2015 Bakr was detained for three days in connection with the investigation into the murder of Dana Seetahal, a prominent criminal lawyer who had supervised the sale of Bakr's properties in 2010 and led the prosecution against Bakr for sedition.⁵³ "Nothing has stuck, because it's fabricated," Bakr told the American journalist Danny Gold in 2014. "They list all the charges in a book, and they just throw the book at me ... That's not prosecution, that's persecution!"⁵⁴

\*\*\*

One of the most telling and unnerving details recounted in Pantin's *Days of Wrath* is of Bakr, on day three of the coup, singing along to "Portrait of Trinidad," which many Trinis regard as their true national anthem:

> As [Jones] Madeira [the News Director at TTT] stepped into the General Manager's office, there was Bakr, using the mouth of an AK47 rifle as a microphone, singing along with a popular calypso playing on the radio. It was the old legendary calypsonian, Sniper, crooning, 'Trinidad is my land and to love it I'm proud and glad' ... Bakr, standing behind the General Manger's desk singing into his rifle muzzle that Sunday morning in TTT, was not alone in his sing-along. Two or three other gunmen had joined in, one of them using his rifle butt as a drum, and the other strumming an imaginary guitar on his AK47.⁵⁵

Just days earlier, Bakr and his men had aimed those very same weapons at the heads of the hostages in TTT, and had put them to vigorous use against the army. And now they were behaving like, in Pantin's words, "little boys turning sticks into imaginary guns."⁵⁶ It didn't seem to add up.

In the closing pages of *Days of Wrath*, Pantin wonders if Bakr is crazy. Recalling the moment when, just minutes away from walking out of TTT, the JAM leader had invited all the hostages to dinner at his Murcarapo compound as soon as the whole coup business was over, Pantin wrote: "A shuddering thought went through my mind: he's insane. He's probably been insane for years, but in a place like Trinidad he had appeared just another one of those characters haranguing passers-by in Woodford Square ... proclaiming the End of The World."⁵⁷ "I saw," Pantin continued, "how in this carnival lunacy, this masquerade, it was entirely possible that this character was playing the role of a king."⁵⁸

Bakr, as Pantin describes him, was a fantasist: a "playacting carnival king" who believed in his own hype. A fictive Ayatollah who every time he wanted to make an entrance insisted on being chauffeur-driven through the streets with outriders, just like his idol Muammar Gaddafi had done in Libya.

On the two occasions when I tried to meet Bakr in 2016 I was rebuffed. So I was not able to take the measure of the man in person. But having read thousands of news articles on him, as well as watching hours of TV footage of him speaking, the person he most reminds me of is President Donald Trump. Bakr would no doubt appreciate the comparison: "I have the greatest respect for Trump," he told a radio journalist in 2017, insisting that politicians in Trinidad could learn a lot from the US President. "Imam Bakr, are you serious?," a perplexed Wendell Stephen replied.[59]

Like Trump, Bakr is vainglorious, narcissistic, shameless, and incapable of self-reproach. Both men are seemingly made of Teflon: despite the tsunami of rumor and controversy in which they are constantly embroiled, nothing sticks to them. And just like Trump, Bakr was a master of identity politics, exploiting the fault line of race to win and hold on to political power. Whereas Trump appeals to white Americans who feel disempowered by the status quo, Bakr appealed to Afro-Trinis who felt downtrodden and oppressed by "the system."

"The JAM today is a spent force," the criminologist Daurius Figueira told me, when I interviewed him in early 2016. And I could see that for myself when, later on that year, Fuad Abu Bakr showed me around the compound at Murcarapo. Other than a handful of school children running around and a few battered cars parked outside the mosque, it was deserted. "This place was full, it was a community, people lived here, people were coming in droves," Fuad said, referring to the period just before the attempted coup in 1990. He also spoke wistfully of a period of "communal living, even community justice." "If you had an issue, you came to the imam, and he would send his guys and they would sort it out." Apparently, the JAM would take to the streets in a blue van, meeting out rough justice to drug dealers and other traders in vice. What Fuad neglected to tell me is that after the coup the JAM itself had become an active player in the drug trade, taxing dealers in return for protection.[60] Its members were also involved in shakedowns, kidnappings, and professional killings. By the mid-1990s the JAM was so enmeshed in criminality that it resembled less a religious enterprise than a criminal one.[61]

Around the same time, the group was riven with internal strife, and several core members left, including Bakr's second-in-command Bilaal Abdullah and Nazim Mohammed. While Abdullah left Trinidad for China, quitting Islamic activism altogether, Mohammed sought to establish his own Islamic community in the south of Trinidad in Rio Claro and away from all the drama and violence and *bacchanal* [scandal] that surrounded Bakr.

The JAM may well now be a spent force, as Figueira says, but its dark legacy remains, like a scab that won't heal. This is for two key reasons. First, the events of 1990 served to radically undermine public trust in the T&T state: in its ability not just to control the monopoly of violence in the country, but also to bring to account those who challenge that monopoly.[62] Second, the JAM helped foment the rhetoric of jihad in Trinidad, since it explicitly used this rhetoric to justify the coup. Despite the hollowness of this rhetoric, Bakr was instrumental in helping it take root in Trinidad, where it found fertile soil in the radical milieu surrounding Nazim Mohammed, and where it was taken seriously as a philosophy to live and die by. It was out of this milieu that the Trini ISIS mujahideen emerged.

# 3

# The Jihad Goes Global: ISIS and the Trini Mujahideen

*I'm feeling like I'm still dreaming…I'm thinking like I'm in a dream world…Please, all believers, come to Sham [Syria] as soon as possible. Do not make the shayṭān [devil] hold you back…look at all the little children, they are having fun.*
Zaid Abdul Hamid, Eid Greetings from the<br>Land of Khilafah, August 2, 2014[1]

*We came here to take over this place and implement the sharia [Islamic law]. And after we take the neck off of Assad, we will take the neck off of Trump, inshallah ['if God wills'].*
Zaid Abdul Hamid, Flames of War 2,<br>November 29, 2017[2]

Jürgen Todenhöfer was the first Western journalist allowed to enter ISIS-controlled territory in Syria and Iraq—and make it out alive. "We saw people from all over the world," he said.

> From Sweden, France, the United States. There was a guy from the Caribbean. Very good looking. Very charming. Stylish, *Ray-Ban* glasses. And I said, "What are *you* doing here?" "What have you done before?" He said, "I was just admitted to the court of my country." I asked him, "Are you going to fight or are you going to work in the administration as a lawyer?" He said, "I'm going to do whatever the *caliph* is asking."[3]

Todenhöfer is describing Tariq Abdul Haqq, a brilliant young man who represented T&T in the 2010 Commonwealth Games in Delhi, earning a silver medal in the men's super-heavyweight boxing division.

Tall, muscular, and handsome, Tariq stood out even in Trinidad, where there is no shortage of stand-out people. But he must have cut quite a figure in Syria among all the grisly one-eyed, tin-legged jihadists who had flocked there in support of the caliphate.

Tariq traveled to Syria in December 2014, along with his wife, a woman named Abbey Greene. He was joined by his sister Aliya, who would have also cut quite a figure inside the caliphate were it not for its draconian dress code forbidding women to show their faces (and even hands and ankles) in public. In the one photo I have of Aliya unveiled, she is tall, slim, and attractive.

In the year before he left Trinidad, Tariq had everything going for him. He had just completed his professional training to become a lawyer, having graduated a few years earlier from the University of London. He had the support of a wealthy and well-connected family, and he was on course to follow in the footsteps of his aunt Pamela Elder, a leading defense attorney in Trinidad. Yet none of this seems to have insulated him against the lure of joining the caliphate to fight in a holy war.

Unlike many Western jihadists, Tariq didn't leave a big social media footprint; he was too busy making a mark in the offline world. But he did, up until September 2014, keep a Facebook page, which offers a fascinating, if only very partial, glimpse into his interior world. It doesn't look like a pro-ISIS account. For a start, it isn't adorned with the distinctive black flag of ISIS. There are no gory screenshots from ISIS propaganda videos. There are no hysterical rants about "dirty kuffars" and death-deserving apostates. There are no posts containing "banging" *nasheeds* [hymns]. Instead it is far more interesting. In one post, on May 30, 2014, Tariq briskly warned: "The Devil is constantly using new ways to lead you astray!" Two days prior to this he posted an advert: "Used Samsung Galaxy S3 For Sale. [TT] $1900. (small crack on bottom right corner)." On February 27, 2014, just days before the annual carnival, he cautioned: "If you think life is about partying, you've lost the plot."

Tariq's posts are rarely more than a sentence long and give little away. But what he does say conveys a temperament that is conservative, religious, and serious. He doesn't crack any jokes, just one reference to laughing "for 5 mins strait" at a clip he posted from an American TV game-show called *Family Feud*. "Name something that follows the word 'pork,'" the host asks. "Cupine," replies one of the guests, smiling at his acuity.

On November 3, 2013, Tariq updated his profile picture: he is clean-shaven and wearing a pale grey blazer, with the top-button fastened, and a white shirt and salmon pink tie. He is looking straight into the camera, with his mouth closed. There is not even a ghost of a smile on his face. One of his Facebook friends comments, "Great you look all business like, keep it up bro." Another says, "You look very handsome there boy." That last comment was made by Aneesa Waheed, the daughter of Imam Nazim Mohammed, the religious leader at the center of the ISIS network in T&T. In April 2018 an Iraqi court in Baghdad sentenced Aneesa to twenty years imprisonment for joining ISIS.[4]

Tariq's sister's Facebook page is far more predictably ISIS, although I doubt the selfie she posted on October 11, 2015, would be tolerated by the group's morality police. In it Aliya is wearing a black *niqab*, but it's her heavily made-up eyes that take center stage. It's a picture that announces, simultaneously, "look how modest I am!" and "look how beautiful I am!"

On August 19, 2015, Aliya posted another intimate portrait of herself, but this time she is with someone else. He is tall, bearded (of course), and powerfully built: this is her new Trini husband Chris Lewis (AKA "Figman"). The picture has been edited so that it looks like a black-and-white pencil-drawn sketch. A red love heart is superimposed over the space where Aliya's chest meets Chris's. It is mawkish and infantile, the kind of thing a teenager would post. But Aliya isn't a teenager. She is a woman in her late twenties. And now a widow twice over: her first husband, a Trini named Osyaba Muhammad, was killed in Syria in 2014.[5] And in August 2016, Chris, too, was killed, after a US aircraft bombed the ISIS compound he was guarding.[6] That same month Aliya gave birth to Chris's son.

In another post Aliya shines a vivid light onto her brother's transformation. It is a photo of Tariq in Syria wearing a metallic grey *shalwar kameez*, a black beanie hat and a thick beard. Behind him you can just make out an AK47 propped up against a bare white wall. Below the photo there is just one comment: "*subhanallah* ['glory be to God'] that my boy may Allah shower his *Rahmah* [mercy] on him. (Amee)." This is Aneesa Waheed again, in what may be a reference to Tariq's death.

Unlike her brother, Aliya leaves little or no room for ambiguity in her online posts. She doesn't insinuate her support for ISIS, as many Western ISIS supporters do in their carefully coded online speech; she loudly proclaims it, knowing that there is no way back for her. Two months after Chris's death, and just as the ISIS project in Syria started to seriously unravel,[7] she defiantly posted a photo of an ISIS fighter planting an ISIS flag in the sand on a beach.

In another post Aliya embedded a short video clip of a diatribe against America by the US-born radical cleric Anwar al-Awlaki. In the clip, Awlaki is wearing a green camouflage jacket, with a large, gold-plated knife precariously shoved down his pants. He looks and sounds utterly ridiculous, and you wonder how he has become such a touchstone for Western jihadists. Anyway, he says: "The west will eventually turn against its Muslim citizens. Hence my advice to you is this. You have two choices: either *hijrah* or *jihad*. You either leave or you fight." "Sums it up for me …," Aliya comments above the video.

Aliya's worldview is monochrome and Manichean, predicated on a distinction between righteous Muslims, who are good, and non- or deviant Muslims, who are evil. It is also a deeply paranoid one, believing that Muslims everywhere are under grave threat and that the only choice is to fight back and remake the world in accordance with the principles of "true" Islam—i.e., the fringe version of the faith promulgated by ISIS. Above all, it is otherworldly, focused on the hereafter, not the here-and-now, which Aliya contemptuously refers to as the "*dunya*"—the temporal world, a world of only passing value in her eyes. In August 2014, just weeks away from leaving for Syria, she wrote:

I have been thinking eh, there must be more to life than this ... living pay check to pay check, tryin to make ends meet, living lavishly for what? Some get rob, others lose love ones when the money done, some even begin to lose them during their success cuz u begin to c ppl true colours. U get wat u temporarily want but its still a struggle and for what? When ure dead and gone and leave all this behind on this earth which has no benefit to u in the after life, sometimes causing more harm to u then, and harm to ur family fighting over property, loss of family and even life over money. Poor still poor while u living "nice." How can yall really call this a paradise?

This devaluation of the material world, of the present, is wholly in line with ISIS's worldview, where death, for the righteous, is revered as the entry point to a vastly superior world of eternal bliss and fulfillment. It was also directly at odds with Trinidad's ever fragile sense of itself as veritable paradise on earth.

\*\*\*

In August 2007 the *T&T Newsday* ran a profile on Tariq, then 17 years old and in his second year of A Levels at St. Mary's College, Port of Spain. Entitled "The schoolboy gladiator," it described him as "a disciplined and well-balanced young man" who aspired to a career in Law.[8] No one at that point could have imagined that Tariq would have gone on to become a foot-soldier for one of the world's most violent terrorist organizations—or that he would have died in Syria (he lasted less than six months in the caliphate). The idea would have seemed preposterous, just as it would have seemed outlandish that scores of his fellow nationals would have followed the same perilous path.

The official T&T government figure for the number of T&T citizens who joined ISIS in Syria and Iraq is 130,[9] but this is almost certainly a gross underestimate. Indeed, according to several anonymous national security sources in Trinidad, the true figure is likely to be in the region of 240, which easily places T&T at the top of the list of Western countries with the highest rates of ISIS recruitment.

Two hundred and forty may sound like a trifling number: a mere ripple among the 41,000 or so international citizens from eighty countries who joined ISIS.[10] It is, for example, well below the number of French nationals who went (1,700), and still quite a shortfall from the number of Brits who traveled (760).[11] But T&T, with a population of 1.3 million, is tiny in comparison to France and Britain, both with populations of around 67 million. And even if one were to err on the side of caution and accept the official figure of 130, T&T still comes out top of the list of Western countries with the highest rates of ISIS foreign-fighter radicalization. To put this into context, 130 amounts to 96 individuals per million—a rate that is roughly double that of Belgium, which, according to some estimates, has the highest per-capita rate of foreign fighters in Western Europe.[12]

Implicit in Jürgen Todenhöfer's surprise at meeting Tariq in Syria is the assumption that foreign fighters who join ISIS conform to a type, and that whatever that type is it isn't a good-looking dude with a law degree and a promising career, much less one from a place more readily associated with calypso than the caliphate. It is often assumed, as Marc Sageman has observed, that terrorists are poor or oppressed, or that they are frustrated loners or misfits. Or that they're goons or just plain crazy.[13] But the weight of research in terrorism studies suggests otherwise. There is no single profile of a terrorist. And no one more vividly exemplifies this than Tariq Abdul Haqq.

If terrorists are neither poor nor oppressed, if they are neither loners nor frustrated misfits, and if they are neither thugs nor mentally deficient, then what or who are they? The most common answer in terrorism studies is that they are psychologically ordinary individuals who are activated by moral imperative.[14] This is not a particularly illuminating answer, but it's a useful antiseptic against the hysterical view of terrorists as monsters from another planet;[15] it's also, as far as we can know, true.

ISIS, without question, was (and remains) a monstrous organization which presided over, for a period, a state project that inflicted monstrously cruel acts, including genocide, on thousands of human beings, and although it attracted its fair share of sadists and psychopaths,[16] many of its members were ordinary individuals, both men and women, from a vast range of backgrounds and places, including from countries as disparate as Britain, the Maldives, and of course T&T.

Drawing on news reports, national security sources and other anonymous sources from within the Muslim communities in T&T, I was able to establish the identities of 120 Trini nationals who traveled to Syria and Iraq, creating full demographic profiles for 70 of them. Here is what I can relay:

## Age and Gender

Of the seventy individuals in the database, 34 percent are male, 23 percent are female, 9 percent are teenagers (age 13–15) and 34 percent are children under the age of 13. Hence the total percentage of minors is 43 percent, while the ratio of adult men to women is 3:2, which places T&T at the top of the list of Western countries with the highest proportion of female ISIS migrants (40 percent).

The average age at time of departure across all forty of the adults is 34; the average age for males is 35, while the average age for females is 33. These averages are unusual compared to those found for other Western ISIS contingents. Researchers Bibi van Ginkel and Eva Entenmann estimate that the majority of British foreign fighters in Syria and Iraq are aged between 18 and 30.[17] Estimates for the average age of their German, Swedish, Dutch, Belgian and American counterparts are (respectively) 26.5,[18] 26,[19] 23.2,[20] 23.8,[21] and 26.9.[22] In other words, adult Trini ISIS migrants (henceforth TIMs) are on average nearly a decade older than their European and American counterparts.

It's not clear what explains this discrepancy, although it's possible that the financial costs of traveling from Trinidad to Syria or Iraq—a trip that would cost around US $2,300—may have prevented younger ISIS supporters in the country from going. Whatever the reasons, the relative maturity of most adult TIMs suggests that however one is to understand the meaning and appeal of the ISIS subculture in Trinidad, it is unlikely to be illuminated by viewing it primarily as a youth revolt.[23]

## Date of Departure

Four Trinis left Trinidad for Syria in 2013: Shane Crawford and his wife, Milton Algernon, and Stuart Mohamed. Between January 2014 and July 2014 a family of five and a lone individual left, while from August 2014 to December 2014 a total of fifty individuals departed. The remainder left between January 2015 and March 2015. It is likely that the spike in departures between August 2014 and December 2014 was prompted by the historic declaration of the caliphate in late June 2014 by ISIS's chief spokesman Abu Muhammad al-Adnani,[24] as well as by the huge international exposure ISIS had attracted throughout the summer of 2014.

## Level of Education

Regarding the level of education of adult TIMs, 70 percent had graduated from secondary school and 25 percent from a tertiary-level institution (including two who had attended the University of Medina in Saudi Arabia). To put this into context, the World Bank estimates, on the basis of data collected in 2010, that the percentage of the population in T&T aged 30–34 with a completed secondary education was 68 percent,[25] while in 2001, when the average adult TIM would have been in their late teens, the participation rate in tertiary education in T&T was just 7 percent.[26] By local standards, then, the educational level of adult TIMs in the database is above the national average for tertiary-level education.

## Occupation

The majority of adults in the sample (55 percent) are unskilled. This number includes most of the females, who were homemakers in T&T, as well as self-employed males, who earned their living farming or driving vehicles for hire. Twenty percent are skilled, 15 percent semi-skilled, and 10 percent professional. Just one TIM was unemployed at the time of his departure for Syria or Iraq. Occupations at the time of departure were startlingly diverse: those leaving included a secondary-school teacher, a truck driver, an agricultural laborer, an auto mechanic, an offshore welder, a marine safety technician, a taxi driver, a building contractor, a cell-phone store owner, a professional footballer, a debt collector, a car salesman, a seaman, and a farm owner.

## Socio-economic Background

The vast majority of these adults—90 percent—can be categorized as middle class, while 10 percent can be categorized as lower class.[27] None of the TIMs were economically impoverished, and indeed quite a few were from the higher echelons of Trinidadian society: two in the database were lawyers (Tariq and his wife), one was a doctor, and another was the son of a wealthy East Indian family. Whatever is driving the foreign fighter phenomenon in T&T, it is not economic marginalization.

## Marital Status

Among the men, nearly 80 percent were married at the time of leaving, while among the women all were married, with the sole exception of an 18-year-old who left with her family. So, among the TIMs for whom we have data, there were no "jihadi brides," and while in the European and North American context the norm was (to use Marc Sageman's terminology) "bunches of guys" leaving, in Trinidad it was bunches of families.

## Number of Converts

In his *Dabiq* interview Shane Crawford, who himself was a convert to Islam, speculated that "about 60 percent of the mujahidin from Trinidad here in the lands of the Caliphate come from Muslim families, with the remaining 40 percent or so being converts."[28] The database supports this line of speculation. Of the forty adult TIMs, 42.5 percent are converts, while 37.5 percent were born into the faith; information on faith at birth for the remaining 20 percent was not available. This reflects an established pattern in foreign fighter cohorts from other Western countries, which is that converts, constituting just a tiny percentage of the total population of Muslims in those countries, are substantially overrepresented.[29] Van Ginkel and Entenmann estimate that among foreign fighters from those European countries with higher numbers of such fighters, between 6 percent and 23 percent are converts.[30] Yet no other country comes even close to the percentage of converts seen in the T&T case. However, it should be noted that while converts are estimated at around 1–2 percent of the total Muslim population in most European countries, in T&T they constitute around 28 percent of the total Muslim population.[31]

The overrepresentation of converts in the TIM contingent lends support to the view that converts are particularly vulnerable to radicalization, either because of their lack of grounding in Islam or because owing to their marginality from both the new faith community into which they have converted and the former community out of which they moved, they are susceptible to the recruitment pitches of radical preachers offering belonging and righteous authenticity.[32]

## Criminal Record

Thirty percent of the sample had a criminal record or had been involved in criminal activities prior to their departure, while the majority—70 percent—did not and had not. This is broadly in line with research on European foreign fighters: roughly 20 percent of Belgian and Dutch foreign fighters were suspected of criminal activity prior to leaving for Syria/Iraq,[33] while for Italy 21 percent of foreign fighters had a criminal record,[34] and for Spain one-third did.[35]

The majority of TIMs with a criminal record or suspected involvement in criminal enterprises were men (83 percent). The seriousness of the offenses for which they were charged varies, ranging from common assault to drug dealing and murder. The two women with criminal records were jointly charged with their husbands for possession of illegal arms and ammunition. It is striking that the first cohort of Trinidadians which left for Syria in late 2013 were all (with the exception of Crawford's wife) fugitives who faced murder charges in T&T.

## Place of Residence and Mosque Affiliation

In the main, TIMs come from three areas in Trinidad: Rio Claro, Chaguanas, and Diego Martin. The majority—nearly 70 percent—lived in Rio Claro before they mobilized for Syria/Iraq, on or near the Boos Settlement Muslim community led by Nazim Mohammed.

Many TIMs attended Salafi mosques (of which there are fewer than five out of a total of eighty-five mosques in T&T). Some were affiliated with more than one mosque. Crawford and his wife Jamelia Luqman, for example, frequented three: Masjid Ul Khaleefah in Longdenville (Chaguanas), Masjid Us Sunnah in Barataria in the north-west, and Masjid Umar Ibn Khattab in Rio Claro, while Milton Algernon attended both Masjid Umar Ibn Khattab and Enterprise Community Masjid (Chaguanas).

This high degree of geographic clustering is mirrored in ISIS mobilizations elsewhere,[36] and lends further support to the thesis that the key to understanding radicalization and foreign fighter mobilizations lies in tracing the social networks that bind violent extremists together. At the same time, it also lends further support to skeptical voices which challenge the wisdom of focusing so much research attention on online radicalization and extremist "virtual spaces"—not because these spaces are unimportant, but because the relationships that matter most in violent radicalization are conducted in physical spaces in or near to social settings where people live.[37]

Research on ISIS foreign fighters from Western Europe and North America shows that although there is no single profile of an ISIS foreign fighter, there are definite patterns: Western ISIS foreign fighters are typically young (early to mid-twenties), lower-class, second-generation Muslim males from urban areas.[38] Many studies also find that Western ISIS foreign fighters tend to be poorly educated and had become radicalized in social environments outside of mosques.[39] The typical Trini ISIS adult traveler, by contrast and as the data above shows, is a married, financially secure Muslim male or female of Trini background in his or her mid-thirties; and they are likely to be a parent, a resident of a rural area, and a member of a mosque. This not only deviates from the European and American norm, it also confounds explanations of radicalization that depend on the marginalized status of diaspora Muslims in ethnically segregated urban ghettoes.

***

Experts on foreign fighter radicalization make a distinction between "push" and "pull" factors:[40] between what is attractive or felt to be attractive about ISIS that "pulls" people to join it and what is prohibitive or felt to be prohibitive about the joiners' own society that "pushes" them to search for radical alternatives. "Pulls" include the implementation of sharia, the privileging of martial and heroic values, moral absolutism, spiritual salvation, solidarity, the prohibition on free mixing of the sexes, and zero tolerance of same-sex relationships, whereas "pushes" encompass militant secularism, soulless materialism, sexual permissiveness, racial discrimination, and other perceived injustices, poverty, multiculturalism, moral relativism, feminism, military intervention in Muslim-majority countries, democracy, and boredom.

If the Trini ISIS mujahideen were "pushed," what were the relevant pushing mechanisms? And if they were "pulled," what were the relevant points of attraction?

I have spoken with countless Trinis, both Muslim and non-Muslim, who are simply at a loss to explain why their fellow nationals joined ISIS. It was a mystery to them why anyone would want to leave Trinidad, let alone join a terrorist organization in a far-off foreign land beset with interminable and internecine conflict and war. But some were certain: it was the loot, the mighty dollar—that was the primary pulling mechanism. Probably, these Trinis had watched or heard about a local TV news report which relayed the claim that ISIS was paying its foreign fighters $1000 a day.[41] Many Trini Muslims I spoke to repeated this exact figure. But it was the fakest of fake news: foreign fighters were not getting paid $1000 a day; they were not even getting paid $1000 *a month*, as King Abdullah II of Jordan had claimed in September 2014.[42] In fact, the more accurate figure was about $400–$600 a month.[43]

But even if it was true that ISIS foreign fighters were being handsomely remunerated for their services, why would relatively well-off Trinis uproot their families and risk their lives decamping to a warzone just to make some extra cash? It didn't make any sense. They already had money, and if they had wanted to make more of it, they had every opportunity to do so in Trinidad.

If they were not motivated by money, what were they motivated by? In a perceptive discussion of human values and rationality, the German social theorist Max Weber wrote of "persons who, regardless of possible costs to themselves, act to put into practice their convictions of what seems to them to be required by duty, honor, the pursuit of beauty, a religious call."[44] This seems to be a more or less accurate description of TIMs, minus the reference to the pursuit of beauty. More specifically, what seems to have "pulled" Trinis to the Islamic State was a conviction that it was the right or necessary thing to do, a matter of honor and duty, indeed a religious calling that they were obligated to follow. It was a conviction that the Islamic state was the true paradise that Trinidad claimed to be but was not: a pristine society of faith free of corruption, deviance, and worldly temptation. Conversely, what seems to have "pushed" them was a profound spiritual disaffection from the very best that Trinidad had to offer, which was a decent life of tranquility and ease on a tropical island that they came to see as sexually permissive, corrupt, and lacking in any real value—a sort of anti-paradise.

"Syria," said 34-year-old Ziyad Mohammed, "is better than Trinidad because it does not have such obscene acts as homosexuality and alcohol."[45] Mohammed, who left for Syria in August 2014 and recently surfaced in a Kurdish-run prison in northern Syria, has denied that he fought for ISIS (he was a mechanic, he insisted) or that he knew about the beheading of Western hostages when he left to join the group. But he clearly maintains a contemptuous attitude toward the country of his birth and, like many other TIMs, was desperate to leave it because of this.

In fact, to listen to the testimony of the Trini ISIS Mujahideen you would think, if you didn't know any better, that T&T is a veritable sewer of vice and moral depravity that was not merely repugnant to decent Muslims but intolerant toward their faith. Take career extremist Zaid Abdul Hamid, who appeared in an all-Trini official ISIS video released in November 2015.[46] Sitting at a river's edge alongside his three young children, he said: "In T&T ... You cannot practice your *deen* [religion or belief] 100%. And it was [this] yearning for me that I knew I had to leave this land [T&T] ... I cannot sit and watch my children grow up in this land in which they cannot practice their Islam 100%."

It was a ludicrous claim, all the more so because of Hamid's utter ineptitude in attempting to verbalize it. Throughout his monologue, a portly and dry-mouthed Hamid is assailed by a squad of flies. His face is the apotheosis of strain and agitation, as though he is working very hard at repressing the urge to defecate. Maybe he *was* repressing the urge to defecate, or maybe he was just having difficulty at simultaneously recalling his lines and palming off the flies from his face. But even more incredible than Hamid's baseless assertion that he couldn't fully practice his Islamic faith in T&T was his weirdly Arabized Trini accent. Everyone I spoke to in Trinidad who saw the video mentioned this, with pained embarrassment, ashamed not only that a Trini would join ISIS, but that they would speak to the world in such a bastardized Trini tongue.

Hamid was one of the sixteen men arrested during the state of emergency [SOE] in 2011. He was also a member of the Al Khaleefah mosque in Longdenville, where Shane Crawford often prayed, and an associate of Abdullah el-Faisal, a Jamaican cleric who is currently facing charges in the United States for allegedly acting as a facilitator for ISIS.[47]

Within days of his release from detention during the SOE, Hamid spoke to the *T&T Guardian*, professing his innocence. "Hamid denied being a radical Muslim or a friend of the detainees," the report noted, referring to the other Trini Muslims who had been arrested with him on suspicion of plotting to kill the prime minister.[48] The report also recorded the following: "He is now claiming that questions are being asked about him by Caucasian men. Hamid feels the men—who have been snooping around his Longdenville home—are working with the Central Intelligence Agency to unearth more information to pin the assassination plot on him."[49] "Everybody watching me now," he told the paper, "I have no doubt that if I remain alive I will always be hunted and persecuted," poor Hamid added, exhibiting a trait that all violent Islamists seem to share—namely, self-pity.[50] (A far more streamlined Hamid was captured by the Syrian Democratic Forces (SDF) in northern Syria in early January 2019.[51])

The ISIS video in which Hamid appears also features the testimony of Sean Parson (AKA Abu Khalid al-Amriki[52]). "Even though I had a very comfortable life in Trinidad," he says, "there was something telling me that I don't belong in this place." Parson didn't elaborate on why he didn't belong, but he did say that he had "always wanted to join my brothers who are fighting towards the establishment of this *deen*, because this is one of the noblest of deeds—fighting for the victory of this religion."

Not much is known about Parson's pre-ISIS life. But it didn't take him long to make his mark in Syria, becoming a key figure in ISIS's network of English-speaking, Raqqa-based recruiters. Dubbed "the Legion" by the FBI, its main business was propaganda and incitement. And for a period it was terrifyingly effective, remotely guiding several ISIS plotters in the United States to carry out attacks there.[53]

Parson was an especially active Twitter user, using his numerous accounts to disseminate ISIS's message—and to post self-portraits, including one that shows him caressing a white kitten.⁵⁴ I implore you to check it out: He is dressed in all black and—following jihadi convention—has a weapon pointing at his crotch. He looks every bit the ISIS *mujahid*: sentimental, serious, and slightly bonkers. Parson was also using Twitter's private messaging service to directly communicate with supporters outside of ISIS-controlled territory in Syria and Iraq. One of these was Keonna Thomas, a 32-year-old mother of two from Philadelphia. According to court records, Parson had married Thomas over Skype and had encouraged her to join him in Syria.⁵⁵ Ever the sweet-talker, Parson told Thomas, via an electronic messaging service, "U probably want to do Istishadee with me."⁵⁶ *Istishadee* isn't one of the many Trini expressions for shagging or *bullin*, but refers to a suicide bombing. To this, Thomas gushingly replied: "That would be amazing … a girl can only wish."⁵⁷ Ramping up his charm offensive, Parson later confided to his wife-to-be: "If I married U and u betrayed me … if my wife comes and it turns out she was a spy after all these yrs … I will personally behead her."⁵⁸

Thomas, who was arrested by the FBI the day before she was due to board a plane to Barcelona, from where she had planned to go to Turkey and onto to Syria,⁵⁹ was also in communication with Abdullah el-Faisal, who may have introduced her to Parson.⁶⁰ Whether or not Parson "virtually" consummated his marriage to Thomas remains unclear, but given how prodigiously active he was online you wouldn't bet against it.

In July 2015 Parson even gave an interview to an Australian journalist, who quizzed him about life in the caliphate. "Imagine living in a drug free society," he told her. "No gays. No prostitution. Where you can leave your business open and no one touches your stuff."⁶¹ Was this a reference to the Sodom and Gomorrah that is modern-day T&T, where the streets crawl with gays and prostitutes? Actually, no it wasn't because in socially conservative T&T gays are largely closeted and prostitution isn't exactly out in the open. And of course no one in the caliphate, except fellow ISIS members, would be stealing Parson's

AK47. It was standard ISIS propaganda; it was just laughable coming from a T&T citizen.

Asked whether he had participated in any beheadings, Parson answered: "Yes, a few days ago on the battlefield in Al-Hasakah [a city in Syria with a large Kurdish population]."[62] Two months after giving this interview, Parson was killed in a drone strike.[63] In one of his last tweets he stated, perhaps in anticipation of his own fate, "You fly a remote control plane halfway across the world to kill an enemy that you are to [sic] coward to meet face to face."[64]

\*\*\*

The discourse on "push" and "pull" factors is really a discourse about motive. Why did they leave? This is the core question that dominates press coverage of ISIS foreign fighters from the West: how could these seemingly normal people, with decent lives, sacrifice it all for a death-cult in Syria and Iraq? Or at least this is how the question is customarily posed, usually in a tone of anguish and bewilderment. It is also the most intractable question you can ask about foreign fighters, and the one most acutely vulnerable to polemical gerrymandering. It is intractable because you can't see a motive and because, often, people do things without knowing why, or without being able to articulate why. As scholar John Horgan put it, "The most valuable interviews I've conducted [with former terrorists] have been ones in which the interviewees conceded, 'To be honest, I don't really know.'"[65]

And it is acutely prone to polemical manipulation because people are liable to invoke self-serving motive-explanations for the things they do and are especially defensive if their actions are questionable or controversial. Of course Parson says that he felt that he didn't "belong" in Trinidad. Of course he says that he came to Syria to defend the honor of Islam. Of course Crawford tells his mother that he came to Syria to help his "Muslim sisters" and protect them from rape and death. Of course Abdul Hamid laments that he didn't have religious freedom in Trinidad. Of course these men—all cold-blooded killers—invoke motives that serve to rationalize and even ennoble their actions. But this doesn't tell us anything about their actual motives, although it tells us a great deal about their urgent need for justification.

A more manageable but no less important question about foreign fighters is not why they joined the jihad in Syria and Iraq, but *how* they joined. This is really a question about recruiters and facilitators: the people who turn wannabe jihadists into real-life ones. It is also, more broadly, about networks, resources, and ideology.

One of the most striking features about the Trini ISIS mujahideen is just how networked it was. Everyone in it was connected to everyone else. They all knew each other, because they either were related or were friends. It was mothers and daughters, fathers and sons, brothers and sisters, husbands and wives. And when the men started getting killed in Syria and Iraq their widows married the remaining male Trini fighters. In all, at least twenty-six Trini families went to live in the caliphate. It is difficult to know how each member of the Trini ISIS mujahideen radicalized, given that so much about them remains hidden or unknown. But the crucial, transformative moment in their life stories was their exposure to the ISIS network in Trinidad, which would have provided them with the social, ideological, and material support for embracing ISIS's worldview and journeying to ISIS-controlled territory in Syria and Iraq. None self-radicalized.

At the center of the network was imam Nazim Mohammed. Not only was he a leading spiritual authority within the network, as well as a revered and feared veteran of the 1990 attempted coup; he also presided over his own quasi mini-caliphate on the settlement he owns in the rural town of Rio Claro in the southeast of the country, and where he still lives. It was from here that the majority of the Trini ISIS mujahideen came or spent some time.

In media interviews, Mohammed has denied any association with ISIS, yet some fifteen members of his family left to join the group in Syria and Iraq, including his daughter Aneesa, his son-in-law Daud Waheed, and several of his grandchildren. Mohammed is also related to Emraan Ali, who married his daughter Sulaimah and helped finance his mosque. In September 2018 the US Department of the Treasury named and sanctioned Ali, along with fellow Trini national Eddie Aleong, as a financier of ISIS.[66] (Ali left for Syria, with his family, in March 2015; his current status is unknown.)

***

In almost every interview I carried out in Trinidad the name of Nazim Mohammed was mentioned. And almost always the same assertion was made: Nazim is the main man. The recruiter. The key link to ISIS in Syria and Iraq.

It is an assertion that Nazim himself vigorously disputes. In October 2014 he told the *T&T Sunday Express*: "I am hearing that I am a recruiter. But I am not sending anyone there [to Syria and Iraq]. Perhaps they think I am a recruiter because I am outspoken, you see, but I am not recruiting anyone."[67]

Nazim's world is so small and self-contained that it is hard for outsiders to penetrate it. Only a few of his associates and acquaintants were willing to speak to me about him, and never other than under condition of anonymity. "Trinidad is small, and you can be taken out easily," one source told me, reiterating a concern that many others voiced to me over speaking on the record about ISIS in Trinidad.

Only one person—let's call him Bilal—properly opened up about Nazim. A former resident of Rio Claro, Bilal, who is in his early sixties, has known Nazim for decades. He invited me to his house, where we had juice and watermelon. "He's a very devoted fella," Bilal said, "self-taught, very learned in the Islamic sense, and very well versed in the Quran and *Hadith*. He's a purist. And he's been that way for most of his life." Nazim's family, according to Bilal, first came to Trinidad in the late 1800s with the other indentured laborers from India. They were farmers who started out dirt poor, but by the time Nazim reached adulthood they had become well-off. Well-off enough to buy the land in Rio Claro on which Nazim's settlement, including his mosque, sits.

Did it surprise Bilal that so many of those Trinis who went to Syria and Iraq lived on Nazim's settlement or visited his mosque? It did not. The ISIS "philosophy," he said, was a "continuation" of Nazim's own.

Does he think Nazim also helped facilitate the migrations of some or many of those who left Trinidad for Syria and Iraq? "My own guess is yes. He has those contacts." To underline his point, Bilal claimed that Nazim had known Adnan el Shukrijumah, a high ranking al-Qaeda leader who was killed in a raid in Pakistan in 2014.[68] El Shukrijumah, who lived in Trinidad as a child in the 1980s and whose Guyanese father used to proselytize in the country, visited Trinidad just prior to the September 11 attacks in 2001, rooming in Chaguanas at the home of a man named Zainool Ali, chairman of Islamic Relief Centre. "He just visited friends, had dinner, went to the beach,"[69] Ali told the *T&T Guardian*, as though he was referring to a son who had just returned from university instead of a terrorist-in-the-making. Bilal told me that el Shukrijumah had also stayed "by" Nazim at the Boos settlement.

Bilal clearly admires Nazim, describing him as a principled and dedicated leader of his community, where "he's loved and respected—and feared." He lingered on that last word, so I probed him further on it. Nazim, a diminutive figure now in his late seventies, certainly doesn't *look* scary, but I guess looks can be deceiving. "He offers total protection for the whole community," Bilal went on, explaining, "if you have an orange or a mango tree in your yard you have no worry, no one stealing from you." How does Nazim enforce this, I asked? "He has a whole contingent of young men, who you don't want to mess with," Bilal replied. Or at least Nazim *did* have such a contingent, before they all left for Syria and Iraq. Men like Crawford, Algernon, Chris Lewis, and Stuart Mohamed, all serious muscle, all killers, all now dead.

And Nazim's split with Yasin Abu Bakr? Did Bilal have any thoughts about this and the relationship between these two men of faith with larger-than-life reputations? "He [Nazim] wanted to promote true Islam, according to his view, and he felt very strongly that Yasin Abu Bakr and his group were more concerned with worldly matters than with *dawah* [proselytizing], so that's why they broke." In a research paper on the Jamaat al Muslimeen, published in the *British Journal of Criminology*, the sociologist Cynthia Mahabir explicitly addresses some of these "worldly matters," describing how the JAM, after 1990, transformed itself from an idealistic social movement—"a fraternity of 'revolutionary men of Allah'"—into a criminal operation.[70] According to the analyst Chris Zambelis, the JAM, from at least the mid-1990s on, became embroiled in "gangland-style slayings, narcotics and arms trafficking, money laundering, extortion, kidnapping, and political corruption."[71] Bilal also cited Bakr's personal acquisition of a large plot of land in Rio Claro as a source of tension between the two men: Nazim, according to Bilal, didn't approve of the way in which this was done.

I told Bilal that I wanted to go down to Rio Claro and interview Nazim. He leaned back and whistled. "He will assume you're a CIA plant," he said. Then he gave me a warning: "When you speak to him, you can't possibly think that all the evil things that have been said about him can be right. This fella is so sweet, so mellifluous, so self-effacing. But he's vicious, he's uncompromising. Watch *yuhself*."

As I waved Bilal goodbye and trudged off toward the *Maxi*-stand, my abiding thought was whether I could possibly believe all the things *Bilal* had told me about Nazim. Trinis do love to talk and gossip and exaggerate. How much of what Bilal had said was accurate and how much of it was unfounded rumor? I needed to see Nazim myself to try and find out. So I took a trip to Rio Claro to meet him, curious to know if he would open up to me. Would he maintain the poker face, or would he lower the mask?

# 4

# The Imam

*It's official—Rio Claro imam Nazim Mohammed has confirmed that his daughter Anisa Waheed Mohammed and two granddaughters have each been sentenced to 20 years in jail by Iraq's courts for alleged association with the Islamic State (ISIS).*

*T&T Guardian*, Facebook, May 5, 2018

*While I feel it for their family why is this news! They choose to leave this paradise to go to a country where others are leaving in droves smh [shaking my head]! There are other pressing issues locally to deal with.*

Catrina Squires-Singh, Facebook Comment Post, May 5, 2018

When, on April 30, 2018, Aneesa Waheed entered the dock at the Central Criminal Court in Baghdad she cut a dejected figure. Dressed in a blue hijab, glasses, and a standard issue pink jail-house *abaya*, she told the judge that she had come to Iraq with her family to help build and expand a divinely mandated Islamic state free of filthy infidels and lowly apostates. "We came in support of our *caliph*, Abu Bakr al-Baghdadi, to defend the caliphate and to slaughter those dirty Shia pigs." Actually, no, that wasn't what she said, and there would be no index-fingered ISIS salute brazenly raised as she said it. She would have said and done those things back in 2014 when ISIS was in the ascendance and looked unstoppable. Of course she would have, just like all the other ISIS loudmouths and blowhards had done over social media back in those heady first months of the establishment of the caliphate in June 2014. But this was April 2018: almost a year since ISIS had lost Mosul,[1] the seat of its caliphate in Iraq, and Aneesa, like hundreds of other foreign ISIS wives caught trying to flee the country by Iraqi government troops, was facing the prospect of life behind bars for illegally entering Iraq and joining a terrorist organization. So, no, she wouldn't be uttering those words today, nor would she be making the *tawhid* [oneness of God] sign in support of *al-Dawla* ["the state"]. This, in fact, is what she said:

> I had watched ISIS videos with my husband and two daughters and we decided we wanted to go and be part of an Islamic society. I did not know it was a warzone. When we arrived, all we saw was Iraqis killing Iraqis, Russians killing Russians, and Turks killing Turks. I did not find Islam here. Your honour, I'm just a housewife, I stayed at home with my daughters the whole time.[2]

Which wasn't entirely false: Aneesa *was* a housewife, both in Iraq and back in Trinidad, and she probably had watched a lot of ISIS videos and wanted to start over in what she was convinced was a truly Islamic society. But she was far more than "just" a housewife in Trinidad; she was also a prominent and active member of the ISIS network there, according to an anonymous source in the Strategic Services Agency (SSA), T&T's equivalent of the FBI. And she would have known that Iraq was in a state of war and turmoil when she entered it with her family in January 2015. How could she not have known? Granted, Trinidad is far from Iraq and Syria, and the décor in even its top hotels is still stuck in the 1970s, but it's hardly some remote outpost disconnected from the rest of the world. Aneesa was active on Facebook, for pity's sake. And she was not a stupid woman. She knew full well that Iraq and Syria were in a state of ongoing war and turmoil. And, just like every other ISIS supporter, she would have probably followed each skirmish with assiduous interest, like a devoted football fan following her team, cheering on each victory and minimizing every defeat. And she would have known all about "Jihadi John" and the slaughtering of the Western hostages, as well as ISIS's cut-throat jihad against the Shia in Iraq. And she would have known, too, about the sexual enslavement of the Yazidis. She would have known about all these things because in mid-late-2014 the entire world's news media were talking about little else. No, Aneesa was not stupid. And neither was the presiding judge in Iraq's Central Criminal Court: he gave her twenty years.

It was a severe sentence, given that Aneesa hadn't fought on the battlefield or (as far as we know) physically harmed anyone. Her offence, rather, was her devotion to an idea and a fantasy. On June 29, 2014, ISIS spokesman Abu Muhammad al-Adnani spoke, in a now historic speech, of "a hope that flutters in the heart of every *mujahid* [fighter]."[3] He was referring to the caliphate, adding, triumphantly: "Now the dream has become a reality."[4] Or at least it must have seemed like that when Aneesa, her husband Daud, son Masud, daughter Azizah, and Azizah's two children left Trinidad together on December 29, 2014. But now the dream, for Aneesa and for all the other suddenly contrite ISIS captives, including almost her entire family, had become a nightmare. "I am old, I have diabetes and my health is deteriorating, I am not a threat to anyone," Aneesa told *The Telegraph*'s Josie Ensor, as she sat in the court's holding cell, handcuffed to another woman whose face was hidden behind a *niqab*.[5] "I can't do 20 years in here," she said, her eyes hot with tears. "We're all going to die here, and for what?" Certainly not for the glory of the now defeated caliphate.

As late as April 2016 Aneesa had posted a comment on Facebook, praising the newly updated profile picture of her 16-year-old nephew. At the center of the picture were the capitalized words: "IF YOU WANT TO MAKE A MUJAHID LAUGH THEN THREATEN HIM WITH DEATH." "That is so true boy lol," Aneesa wrote. About a week later, the same nephew posted a photo of an ISIS fighter posing alongside a machine gun. Emblazoned over it were the words, again in hollering, finger-jabbing capitals, "IF DEATH IS WHAT YOU OFFER US THEN KNOW, WE CAME TO DIE." "Subhanallah ['glory be to God']," Aneesa commented. Aneesa, now facing the prospect of death in an Iraqi prison cell, was laughing no longer. Death, it turned out, wasn't what she wanted after all.

She was 51 when she left for Iraq, as was Daud, whose fate currently remains unknown, although rumor has it in jihadi circles in Trinidad that he was executed in mid-2018 by the Kurds in northern Iraq. If it was a midlife crisis, it was a particularly costly one. But of course it wasn't a midlife crisis. It was a spiritual one, prompted by the declaration of the caliphate. And it had affected the whole of Aneesa's immediate and extended family, including her brother Musab and her and Daud's three other daughters Azizah, Aiydah, and Sabirah, who all left Trinidad with their respective husbands and children between September 2014 and March 2015.

Like Aneesa, Azizah, 32, and Aiydah, 23, were jailed for twenty years, having stood trial in the same Baghdad court a week before their mother had received the same sentence in April 2018.[6] As of writing, Sabirah, 29, is currently in detention and awaiting trial.

At the head of Aneesa's family is her father: Nazim Mohammed, the Imam of the Umar Ibn Khattab mosque in Rio Claro. He is one of the few members of Aneesa's family who *didn't* go to Iraq and Syria. In fact, he claims that he didn't even know that his daughter Aneesa and son-in-law Daud had gone to Iraq until Aneesa told him, via telephone a week after they had left. He has also strongly denied that he had anything to do with their decision to join ISIS. Nor could he recall, he told the *T&T Guardian* in 2016, meeting Shane Crawford, who had often prayed at his mosque:

> Maybe I saw him (in the mosque) and thing, but I personally don't know him. I never spoke to him. All I know him is by seeing his photos in the newspapers. Maybe he attended my mosque, I can't remember every face. Maybe he passed through the mosque, I don't know. People would come from all over to attend Juma'ah [Friday Prayer].[7]

In Islam it is forbidden to lie, but lying to *kuffars* for the purposes of defending the faith, according to some Islamic schools of thought, is permissible. When Nazim denied knowing of Aneesa's decision to leave, along with her family, was he engaging in *taqiyyah* [dissimulation]? Or was he simply telling the truth? And, if so, was his authority held in such low regard that Aneesa and the others could leave Trinidad and the faith-based community he had created there for them without even telling him, let alone without seeking his permission, if not approval?

And was he that oblivious to the goings on in his settlement, where his mosque is housed and where most of his family lived, that he didn't notice their preparations to move half way around the world in search of the caliphate in Syria and Iraq?

It doesn't really seem credible. But that, in part, is because Nazim is a veteran jihadist: he had fought in the earlier jihad in Trinidad, where he had proved himself to be a tough, fearless, and uncompromising combatant. This is the journalist Raoul Pantin, describing Nazim in his first-hand account of the attempted coup, where he had been held as a hostage for the entirety of the six days it lasted:

> I put him in his early 50s, a short portly man with gray hair, a gray beard and a smiling kindly face and demeanour. Those traits of goodness made the large automatic rifle in his hand appear incongruous … This old man, an Imam himself, Nazim Mohammed he said his name was, looked tiredly happy, resting up from the gun battle. He seemed pleased to expound on his faith.[8]

Almost thirty years later Nazim is still recognizably the man in Pantin's description, though he is now in his late seventies and no longer portly, and his beard is now fully white. He was in the thick of it when the jihad went local in Trinidad in 1990, but, if his testimony to T&T's press is to be believed, by the time of the Syrian jihad over twenty years later he was completely out of touch, with both world events and affairs closer to home inside his own mosque and settlement.

Since reading about Nazim in the local newspapers I had been curious to meet him, and at the end of the summer in 2018 I got my chance. My friend Azard Ali, a journalist who works for *T&T Newsday*, had planned to go and see Nazim at his settlement in Rio Claro. He was going to talk to him about Aneesa and her children. Would I like to join him? I responded in the affirmative and with enthusiasm. But I wasn't exactly relishing the ride to Rio Claro, where I knew the roads to be bad and more than a little lawless. In Trinidad, on the street, if you walk with purpose and pace you are acutely aware that you are engaging in behavior that is regarded as suspect, if not wholly deviant. And there is some sense to this: only a fool, or an Englishman, would walk with purpose and pace in a country as oppressively humid and hot as Trinidad. Behind the wheel, however, Trinis are an altogether different proposition: speed junkies, for whom giving an inch or merely activating the indicator is a sign of moral weakness. In Trinidad, if you drive with anything less than reckless abandon you are considered a chump, a loser, or very English.

Luckily, the ride down to Rio Claro was uneventful. And for some of the two-hour journey, when I wasn't frantically reminding Azard to keep his eyes on the road, I was able to lose myself in the incredible vistas of dense jungle and bush that open up the further south you go. Beautiful though it is, you wouldn't want to get lost here or breakdown. The meeting with Nazim was to prove far more eventful.

When we pulled up at the Boos settlement, a large area of land (Nazim said it was just 2 acres, although it looked much larger) on which the mosque sits along with thirty or so houses, Nazim came out to greet us. He was dressed in an off-white *shalwar kameez*, flip-flops, and a dark gray prayer hat. He looked fit and spritely on his feet, and his beard was long, thick, and white. After a protracted round of introductions and salutations, he gave us a brisk tour of the mosque, a rather drab concrete building containing a small classroom, a kitchen, male and female wash-rooms, and a narrow staircase leading to a large and luminous green-carpeted prayer room. As we walked together Azard told Nazim who I was and how I had helped one of Nazim's associates contact the court in Baghdad to check up on Aneesa. I said very little, but was struck by the physicality of Nazim, who, though a good 4 or 5 inches shorter than me (I'm 5' 10"), made me feel like I was the shorter man. He led us to a dark, windowless office where we were to conduct the interview. Before we entered we all took off our shoes. I was thankful that earlier that day I had remembered to wear a proper pair of socks.

Nazim was accompanied by a young black assistant, no older than 25, who wore a Saudi-style *keffiyeh*. As we sat down, I further elaborated on my credentials as a university lecturer, keen to dispel any impression that I was working with the CIA or FBI. A police officer had told me that Nazim, who has a T&T special branch officer assigned to him, is cautious about the prying eyes of the intelligence services, and since the last white faces to visit his mosque were probably officers working for the FBI, I felt a particular pressure to appear as unspooklike as possible.

As it turned out, Nazim showed little interest in my spiel, and got straight down to business. "Right now we want to highlight this issue," he said. By "this issue" he wasn't referring to the illegal entry of well over 200 Trinis into Iraq and Syria for the purposes of joining a fledgling Islamic state that aspired to erase the borders of those two countries and overthrow the existing power structures within them. No, he was talking about the issue of the imprisonment of Aneesa and her children—his grandchildren—in Iraq. Aneesa's trial lasted less than 8 minutes, and were it not for Josie Ensor, who acted as a translator, she wouldn't have even understood what the judge was asking or telling her. Aneesa's two other daughters were similarly dispatched with a disregard for even the minimum standards of due process.

Were it not for "this issue" Azard and I wouldn't have got within a mile of Nazim's compound, let alone got to look around the joint. And even then I had to be vouched for by a fiercely devout Muslim— my friend Umar Abdullah—who wants to create an Islamic state in Trinidad and who is rumored to have fought against the Soviets in Afghanistan in the 1980s. And it no doubt didn't hurt that Azard is a Muslim with whom Nazim is on good terms.

Suspicious of outsiders, Nazim is an intensely private person. He is unapologetically and refreshingly old school. He doesn't use a computer (according to his assistant) or engage in social media, and he doesn't crave public attention, unlike the JAM leader Yasin Abu Bakr, whom Nazim once swore an oath of loyalty to. Indeed, he has given just a handful of interviews to the local news media, not because he wanted to, but because he felt he needed to. And he categorically refuses to participate in the politics of T&T, not because the country's brand of politics is particularly corrupt, dirty, and undignified, which it incontrovertibly is, but because he is theologically opposed to the very idea of democracy, believing that it is at odds with the concept of *tawhid*, according to which God's law supersedes man-made law.

So I knew just how precious an opportunity it was to interview Nazim, and to take the measure of this enigmatic man of faith. Only you don't really interview Nazim. You ask him questions, and he erects a wall of rhetoric to deflect everything you put his way. But talk to him long enough and cracks start to appear in the wall.

Azard asked Nazim whether he had been in contact with Aneesa or any of his grandchildren. "The only one I have communication with is Sabirah," he replied, clarifying that they speak via cell phone about once a week. Sabirah is currently in detention in Iraq and has yet to be tried. "How old is Sabirah?," Azard asked. Nazim dodged the question, and instead spoke about how some Western governments—he singled out Norway—were "making representations" in Iraq to bring back their citizens stranded there. Before the interview, Nazim had mentioned in passing that Sabirah was a medical doctor. Azard now pressed him further on this. "She did her medical degree at Mount Hope here?," he asked, referring to the women's hospital near UWI. Nazim: "Yeah, she qualified." Azard: "She used to work at the hospital?" Nazim: "Nah." Azard: "How old she is?" "Alright boy!," Nazim protested, clearly uncomfortable with Azard's quick-fire style of questioning. Undeterred, Azard asked: "Did she have a job over there?" Nazim: "Yeah, she used to work in different places." Azard: "Was she married?" Nazim: "Yes, her husband is in prison. He's a Guyanese." Azard: "What's his name?" "Umar Kumar," said Nazim's assistant. Azard: "How did Aneesa and her family get to Iraq in the first place?" Nazim: "You see, I didn't know they left ... [mumbles] ... a week after she call me from Iraq. That's all I know." Azard: "You would have questioned her why she left?" Nazim: "No, I didn't ask them much." It was at this point in the interview that Nazim launched into a ten-minute discourse on how Allah wills all things:

> You may understand, you're a Muslim [looking at Azard], you may not understand [looking at me]. You see, here's my concept. I have a

strong, strong belief, and my belief is in the oneness of Allah. *Tawhid.* Everything happen by his will. And my strong belief is in the life hereafter, that this is not the real life. And my strong, strong belief is in *qadā*, decree ... But even though he decree, you can change that decree by *dua* [prayer] ... If he has decree that they [Aneesa and her family] remain there for 20 years in jail then so be it. But then Allah promise if you make *dua* you can change decree ... but nothing can change *pre-destiny.* The best example is Jonah ...

As Nazim continued to expound on the Islamic concept of predestination I felt my mind wander. I glanced around the room, and spotted a book titled *The Levels of Jihad.* I could just about make out a sword on the cover. Did it justify the beheading of infidels, I wondered? I also couldn't help but notice the size of Nazim's hands, big and coarse like shovels. Even now in his late seventies, you wouldn't want to tussle with him—or at least that was the profane thought streaming through my Norman Mailer-like consciousness at the time. And I couldn't help but marvel at the speed at which this old man talked, and just how alert and "on" he was. Even more than this, I was struck by his cast-iron certainty. Here is a man, I thought, who is seldom troubled by the throb of self-doubt. Here is a man who knows he is right about the greatest intellectual and moral questions that life can throw at you. Here is a true believer.

Nazim had probably given this mini-lecture on predestination tens of thousands of times before, so it was impressive that he still managed to imbue it with a keenness and stridency. "A man ejects many millions of seed with his sperm," Raoul Pantin recalled Nazim telling him on day two of the attempted coup in 1990.[9] "But of all those seeds, only one fertilizes the female. That one seed is the will of Allah."[10] Thankfully, there was no talk of male ejaculate when Azard and I spoke with Nazim, but the fatalistic belief that nothing happens unless God wills it was never far from the surface in his frequent efforts to change the subject.

Azard, clearly unmoved by Nazim's oration, then asked, referring to Aneesa and her family: "So you don't think that by them not telling you that they were going can be viewed as an act of disobedience?"

**Nazim**: No I don't.

**Azard**: You don't feel disrespected at all in any way?

**Nazim**: No, no … I'm a Muslim, the Prophet (*sallallahu alaihi wasallam* ["Praise be upon him"]) always give 40 excuse for you … It's actually a better *ting* that I didn't know.

**Azard**: If Aneesa had told you she was going, what you would have said to her?

**Nazim**: No, I would, you know … Maybe I would have told her they could go across there.

**Assistant**: But it's a hypothetical situation, it didn't happen, so …

**Nazim**: Yeah, it didn't happen, so I wouldn't like to go back on it.

**Azard**: You would have discouraged them?

**Nazim**: No … you see … The Prophet (*sallallahu alaihi wasallam*), whenever he was ask, 'if so and so *ting* happen, what you would do?', he never entered in that.

**Simon Cottee**: But would you have approved of their decision to go? Or would you have condemned it?

**Nazim**: Look, you see, that question is very difficult to understand … I can't really say what I would say, because it's a past *ting, yuh* understand?

**Azard**: So much time has passed since they went. You must have some deep thoughts about why they ended up there.

**Nazim**: Again, I come back to the decree of Allah. The decree of Allah.

It went on like this, back and forth, for some time. I asked Nazim what he thought about the legitimacy of the caliphate. Did ISIS have a divine claim to statehood and rule? "I'm not too up with it," he said. "So I wouldn't be in a position to know." But, he reassured me, and not for the first or last time, "I have full trust in Allah."

After another back-and-forth about what Nazim knew and didn't know, Azard then leaned back on his chair and said, "Nazim, I want to come up here and live, boy. And Simon, he might buy a plot too." Nazim, who doesn't do small talk, replied, looking in my direction, "You got to be a Muslim first." "They have good *doubles* down here?," Azard asked. He was trying to get Nazim to loosen up, and Nazim was having none of it: "Those things are not important." "Let me tell you something," he said sternly, addressing me directly. He was about to launch into lecture-mode again:

> What is important is your faith, *yuh* understand what I telling you? The best of Allah's creation is the human being. Every single *ting* was created to benefit mankind. The sun is rising and setting only because man exists here. The stars, the moon … only because man exists here … Now I have to give you this message, because all who come here I have to give them this message. The FBI came here and I make sure I give them this message. Now the doctrine is the Oneness of the Almighty … He is the creator and He is one. And everything else is his creation. Every single *ting*. He was alone … He took light and created the angels. After he created the angels, he created the *jinns* [a supernatural creature in Islamic mythology] … And then now he took mud, black mud, white mud, yellow mud, different colors of mud, he brought it together and created man …

Nazim went on in this vein for about twenty minutes, and in this time he covered the story of Adam and Eve and gave me the low-down on the hierarchy of the prophets. He spoke at length about the Day of Judgment, when "before our Lord he will give us full justice." And he animatedly described the various unending horrors that await those who nullify Islam and languish in sin and disbelief. "Today," he said, "you coming here is a great opportunity, because on the Day of Judgement you will not be able to say, 'Oh Allah, I never heard about this.'" "When I was interviewed by the FBI," he continued, "I told them the same thing: I say, 'On the Day of Judgment, which is a reality, you'll not be able to say, 'I didn't hear this.'" "So I have no excuses," I said, with a half-smile. "No excuses," Nazim flatly replied.

Anticipating further probing from Azard, Nazim said:

> I have nothing to hide, this is a jamaat. We have five daily prayer, in which I lead the prayer. I'm the imam, the leader. After we finish the prayer we have a Quranic session. Every single morning we do one section of the Quran, in Arabic … On a Monday evening we have class for new Muslims on how to pray and so on. On Tuesday we go out on the street and give people the message. On a Wednesday, in the night,

we have a class on Arabic. On Thursday we have a class on the religion and concepts. On Friday night we have a Quranic session. And every Sunday we cook for the poor, taking food to about 100 homes in the area. Basically, this is our program.

I wondered what Nazim and his followers did in their downtime, if indeed they had any. I couldn't really picture him *liming* or watching a Netflix boxset, much less cracking a joke. And I couldn't help but think about how life at his settlement, as he described it, with all that seriousness and toil going on there, sounded so very unTrinidadian.

Further elaborating on life inside the settlement, he said: "We do not encourage drugs. Not even cigarette here. No marijuana. No coke. No alcohol. No gambling. No play away with woman." Hearing this, I glanced over to Azard, thinking that if he did want to come and live with Nazim he'd have to clean up his act—or at least quit smoking.

"He's the Ayatollah," Bilal, the former resident of Rio Claro, told me. "You don't cross Nazim," he added. And you certainly don't commit *zina* [adultery]—i.e., "play away with woman"—under his watch. Here is Nazim again:

> This brother committed fornication before he marry, and he told me, 'Imam, this bothering me.' So I say, 'you know the punishment for that?' He said, 'yes.' I said, 'What it is?' He said, '100 strokes'. And he came and he take the 100 stroke, and he said, 'I feel free now'. *Yuh* understand? If somebody do something that deserve 10 stroke I give them 10 stroke … We're trying to be good citizen. We don't have no crime here, except for small, small *tings*.

I spoke with Umar Abdullah about Nazim. Umar runs an organization called the Islamic Front, which lobbies on behalf of Muslims and Muslim causes. I first interviewed him in 2016, and since then we have stayed in regular contact. Every time I go to Trinidad I pay him a visit. A decent and gentle man, he is a radical critic of the T&T government and clearly relishes his status as an outsider even among Muslims in the country. In the time that I've known Umar I've never heard him say a bad word about any Muslim, although he has plenty of negative things to say about the misuses of American imperial power. Nazim, he told me, "runs a tight ship." When I asked him about Nazim's insistence that he didn't have any prior knowledge of Aneesa's plans to go to Syria, he praised Nazim's integrity and insisted that he doesn't lie. "Not even to an infidel?," I neglected to ask.

Which does beg the question again, doesn't it? If Nazim is indeed the stern and capable ship-master, how was it that so many could have deserted his ship without him even knowing about it?

It seems to me that there are at least three possible scenarios.

The first is that Nazim not only knew about the departures to Syria and Iraq, but actively encouraged and facilitated them, providing leavers with essential contacts and resources.

The second is that he knew what was going on, but opposed it and was powerless to stop it, in which case he had a mutiny on his hands.

And the third is that while he may have supported some departures, he was opposed to others and did not want his immediate family, on whom he depended for running the settlement at Boos village, to go. Umar Abdullah did suggest to me that Nazim and Aneesa's husband Daud had often clashed, but he didn't say over what. Were Daud and Aneesa the driving force behind the departures at Boos? And did they leave without telling Nazim, who they knew would have tried to stop them from leaving? Or was the main agitator behind the departures Emraan Ali, husband to Nazim's other daughter Sulaimah and financier of Trini ISIS fighters in Syria? Maybe they were all up to their eyes in it, working in concert to funnel Trinis into ISIS-controlled territory in Syria and Iraq. Nazim, for his part, wants it both ways. Speaking to me and Azard he portrayed himself as the master of his community, yet he wants the world to believe that he is blissfully ignorant about the truly life-and-death matters that are going on inside it. The problem for Nazim is that he can't be master and innocent at the same time.

In terrorism studies, scholars make a distinction between "top-down" and "bottom-up" recruitment. According to Thomas Hegghammer, the first refers to "the enlisting of initially sceptical recruits by an appointed recruiter," whereas the latter denotes "the process by which self-radicalized recruits seek out, by their own initiative, a passive recruiter or 'gatekeeper.'"[11] Was recruitment in Nazim's settlement and the wider Rio Claro area, from which the majority of the Trini ISIS recruits came, "top-down" or "bottom-up"? And what role (if any) did Nazim play in this? Unfortunately, nobody outside of Nazim's religious community and the even more closed community of the intelligence agencies who monitor it knows the answers to these two questions. What is clear is that Nazim and the network he created provided the ideological ground for the departures of so many of his followers to Syria and Iraq. Numerous sources who know Nazim told me that he has long been anti-American; they also said that his ideological worldview is broadly consistent with the one espoused by ISIS. Umar Abdullah, who had once shared a house with Milton Algernon on the Boos settlement, described to me not only how the caliphate declaration in 2014 electrified many of Nazim's followers, but also how their prior immersion in the thinking of Abdullah el-Faisal had primed that response. "We used to get a copy of every lecture he [el-Faisal] gave," Umar Abdullah said, "because he had a close relationship with Imam Nazim. And we used to listen to those lectures over and over. And in those lectures there was a lot of radical rhetoric ... A lot of brothers were radicalized as a result of listening to his lectures."

The evolution of Nazim's network remains somewhat of a mystery and few people are willing to talk about it. But its origins are fairly easy to specify: it emerged out of the break-up of the Jamaat al Muslimeen (JAM) after the failed coup of 1990. According to the criminologist Daurius Figueira, the JAM started to unravel as soon as its leaders were arrested and put into custody. The divisions had always been there, he told me, but the pains and solitude of imprisonment brought them right out into the open. The core dispute, between Yasin Abu Bakr and the other leaders in the JAM, most notably Bilaal Abdullah, was over the future direction of the group. By the summer of 1992, when the JAM were given a pardon (this was negotiated as a condition of its surrender during the siege) and released from prison, the group was violently and irremediably split. Bilaal Abdullah left and created his own group; he was to leave Trinidad for China not long after. Around the same time Nazim also broke away from the JAM with the aim of establishing his own community in Rio Claro. I asked him about this and why he felt it was necessary to branch out on his own.

> We started as a little group and became part of the JAM [in 1983], he [Yasin Abu Bakr] became our leader, but part of the agreement that we made with them is that, for we to be with you, Number 1, you, as imam, must lead a five-daily prayer. And Number 2, we don't get involved in no politics or political parties.

According to Nazim, Bakr breached both conditions:

> After the coup, when he came out of prison, he [Bakr] stopped establishing the prayer, he stopped coming to the masjid [in Mucurapo] and leading the prayer. We told him about it, he said he'd address it, he didn't address it, and we called a meeting here [in Rio Claro] and I told him, "listen, we can never carry on with you under this condition", because in Islam the leader have to lead a 5 daily prayer ... This is why we left them [the JAM].

Nazim also made it explicit that he disapproved of Bakr's flirtation with the major political parties in Trinidad (Bakr and his group campaigned for the United National Congress—one of the country's main political parties—in the 1995 General Election). And he was "suspicious," he said, about Bakr's links with Libyan leader Muammar Gaddafi, who helped arm and train members of the JAM.

Nazim was careful to insist that he and Bakr are not enemies, but it was abundantly clear from everything he said about him that he doesn't exactly hold the man in great esteem. And whatever he thinks of Bakr as a Muslim, he obviously doesn't think he has any claim to be an imam. This is not quite *takfir* [the practice of declaring another Muslim an apostate], but it's still a serious charge.

As the interview with Nazim drew to a close, I asked him about Milton Algernon, who used to live at Boos. I was trying to get my head around not just the kind of person Algernon was (a criminal or a religious vigilante or both?) and what activities he was involved in, but also the nature of his relationship with Nazim. "Fareed [Algernon] used to belong to this jamaat, he lived here, I helped him, he was kind of rebellious and eventually he left the community, but I didn't expel him from the community." In Nazim's telling, Algernon left Boos well before he went to Syria, but he didn't leave Rio Claro and rented a house in the surrounding area outside the settlement. "We had a strained relationship because certain things he did I didn't approve of and I made it clear to him, *yuh* understand?" Nazim didn't say what, exactly, had aroused his disapproval. But, according to someone who knew Algernon when he was at Boos, the main cause of tension between Algernon and Nazim was the former's involvement in criminality. Algernon, according to this person—let us call him Ali, not his real name—was involved in gun-running, along with Crawford, Stuart Mohamed, and several other members of Nazim's mosque who later went to Syria.

According to Ali, the break with Nazim was precipitated by a disagreement over how to handle the killing of a 26-year-old man from the Boos settlement.[12] Seeking to avenge his death, Algernon, Crawford, and Mohamed first sought Nazim's blessing. "Imam Nazim told them to stand down," Ali said. But they refused to do so, and on November 24, 2013, Algernon, Crawford, and Mohamed took their revenge.[13] This was the double murder hit in Chaguanas: the ground zero event in the Trini Syrian Jihad. "Islamically," Ali told me, "I have no problem with what they did because they were avenging the death of a Muslim brother, *yuh* understand?" Nazim, when I asked him about this revenge killing, said that he knew nothing about it.

\*\*\*

In 2009 Nazim Mohammed came under the radar of the FBI, when agents visited his mosque prior to the Fifth Summit of the Americas, which took place that year in T&T's capital Port of Spain. "They came here, right here in this masjid. They said their President [Barack

Obama] was coming here and wanted to determine whether I was a threat. Very sophisticated men. Spoke Arabic," Mohammed told the *T&T Sunday Express*.[14]

The authorities in T&T would have known about this visit, just as they would have known about Nazim's proselytizing. Yet it seems they were not sufficiently worried to do anything about it. This is puzzling, especially given the dark history of Islamist activism in T&T—and Nazim's own participation in the 1990 attempted coup. Was some sort of bargain struck between Nazim's group and the T&T state, whereby the former would abide by a "covenant of security," provided the T&T authorities turned a blind eye to their activities? Or was the state just straight-up negligent about the emergent threat then stirring in the south of the country? I decided it was time to contact the intelligence agencies in Trinidad. What did they know about Nazim and the wider ideological milieu that he helped establish and out of which the Trini ISIS mujahideen emerged?

# 5

# Homeland Insecurity

*National Security Minister Edmund Dillon was quoted yesterday as saying Isis poses "no threat to T&T right now" and there's no law to stop them returning. He said if they'd committed international crime, T&T could work with foreign partners to bring them to justice, but "for now they're still T&T citizens."*

"89 Trinis join Isis fighters,"
*T&T Guardian*, November 15, 2015

In August 2018 a former member of an intelligence agency in T&T agreed to speak to me about ISIS networks in the country, but only on condition of anonymity. It was under his watch that over 140 Trinis had gone to Syria and Iraq between late 2013 and early 2015. Let's call him Peter, a muscular Trini in his late forties. I'd arranged to meet him in a conference room on UWI campus in St. Augustine.

Peter looked more like a bouncer than a spook, and when we shook hands his vice-like grip conveyed an impression that physical strength and courage were attributes that he particularly admired. Peter, obviously, could take care of himself; he also took some care in signaling to the world that he could take care of himself. This is a standard male vice, to be sure. But it's also an understandable reflex in a culture in which any sign of weakness is seized on and mercilessly taken advantage of. You wouldn't want to try it on with Peter, or at least that's what his presentation of self told you.

It was a challenging and, at times, frustrating interview. Peter told me that he'd read some of my work and that he liked it, although he had an odd way of conveying this information. "I like you're style of writing, but to me it tends to be in line with the status quo, I mean it's not overly interpretational. You write around the theme, but how is it really balanced within the whole socio-philosophical side of where people actually come from?" "To me," he elaborated, "that is one of the greatest misconceptions relative to ISIS, where we tend to lump every situation as one." I had no idea of what Peter was talking about, but I listened all the more intently in the hope that he would arrive at a point that made some sort of sense. "Everybody keep missing the ball," he said. "What's that?," I asked. "ISIS is nothing new," he explained, in a tone that suggested he was making a point that no one had dared utter before. "Freedom fighters, leaving their home countries, and going to the Middle-East, is nothing new." I privately balked at Peter's use of the term "freedom fighter," but I continued to feign interest in his socio-political commentary, because I needed him to keep talking, hoping that he would tell me what I wanted to know: How many Trinis, in his expert view, had joined ISIS in Syria and Iraq? Who was Nazim Mohammed and what was the nature and scope of his influence on the Trini ISIS mujahideen? And what relationship did he have with Shane Crawford, Milton Algernon, and Stuart Mohamed—the first trio of Trinis to go to Syria?

Peter was in no rush to address these questions, preferring instead to raise some probing inquiries of his own to do with epistemology and the social construction of knowledge. As fascinating as this was, I felt the interview was losing focus, so I told Peter that I'd recently interviewed Nazim and found him to be a puzzle. Peter warmed to this theme and told me a cautionary tale about how he'd sent an agent to interview a well-known Islamist in Trinidad. The gist of the story, told with much derisive laughter, was that the agent hadn't done his homework on the Islamist in question and when he reported back to Peter he had no useful information to relay. "Interesting," I said, "but what do you think of Nazim's denial that he has anything to do with ISIS." "What is ISIS?," Peter rhetorically asked. "What do you mean, 'what is ISIS'?," I snapped. "Nazim knows very well that ISIS has been funded by the CIA, which has been supported by all the dissident groups, da der der." "You believe that ISIS is funded by the CIA?," I asked. "Most of the things in the Middle East in terms of the threat structure …," Peter replied, not bothering to finish his point, perhaps sensing my incredulity at his conspiracy-fueled thinking. I had heard this point expressed many times before in interviews I'd conducted with Islamists in Trinidad, but I was surprised and admittedly disconcerted to hear it from a highly experienced former intelligence officer.

I quickly moved on. Did Peter think that Nazim supported Aneesa's decision to go to Iraq with her husband and daughters? "Yes, of course he did," he said. "That is what he wanted ... It's all entwined within his genuine religious belief." I knew from several trustworthy police sources that undercover agents had infiltrated Nazim's mosque and surreptitiously recorded his sermons. Is that how he knew about Nazim's views? Peter said he couldn't say. But he said this: "The majority, if not all, of those who went [to Syria and Iraq] have at one time been affiliated with his [Nazim's] masjid. He and his sons—they are the main coordinators and financiers of those who went." Nazim has two sons, Peter later clarified in an email: one who left to go to Syria, and another who remains in Trinidad and was one of the 114 men in the attempted 1990 coup.[1]

I pressed Peter further on what he knew about Nazim, but he deflected, and returned to the story about the hapless officer with remedial interviewing skills. "You need to stop thinking like a westerner," he said. "You have to think like a Muslim who believes we're in the End Times." I nodded in agreement. But how did Trinis come to believe in ISIS's specific version of this apocalyptic thinking? And who helped the ISIS ideology germinate in Trinidad? On hearing these questions, Peter let out a high-pitched giggle. "You keep saying *ISIS.*" "Ok, *Dawla al-Islamiya* or whatever you want to call it," I replied. He carried on chuckling to himself.

Peter seemed more interested in mocking my questions than in answering them. But I wasn't sure that he didn't still have something useful to say, so I decided to persevere with the interview. I paused for a bit, and then asked him about the number of Trinis who had left for Syria and Iraq during the period when he was tracking them. Was the 130 figure given by the government accurate? Peter let out a *steups*. It was a good one: loud and long-lasting and saturated with contempt. "I would say it's more than that," he said. "I was still ripping out bodies when it was 140-something." This was in early 2015. I asked him again about Nazim's set up in Rio Claro and the number of followers attached to his mosque there, but Peter seemed reluctant to talk about this. But he did disclose that Chris Lewis, Shane Crawford, Milton Algernon, and Stuart Mohamed were part of a single "cell" and that all four men were affiliated with Nazim's mosque.

Chris Lewis, who can be seen doing target practice with a high-velocity weapon in the all-Trini official ISIS video, "was rolling with them all the time," Peter said. I later learned from another law enforcement source that not long before leaving for Syria, Lewis had been investigated by the police for allegedly shooting up the home of a municipal councilor as punishment for her refusal to award contracts to a group of Muslims in Diego Martin.

I then pressed Peter on the 2013 double murder hit in Chaguanas. Peter alluded to "some bad blood" between Crawford's cell and the two men they murdered, but he was reluctant to go into detail about the case. He did, however, open up about Stuart Mohamed, who drove the car that was used in the hit. Prior to speaking with Peter, I'd been closely investigating Stuart for over six months and suspected that he was a high-ranking ISIS external operations planner who went by the *kunya* Abu Isa al-Amriki. I didn't mention this to Peter, since I couldn't be sure whether disclosing my suspicions would discourage him from revealing any information about him. Stuart intrigued me, not just because of his rapid ascendancy through the ranks of ISIS, but because his story was emblematic of a deeper failure of the T&T state to contain the problem of violent extremism on its doorstep.

\*\*\*

I first came across the name of Abu Isa al-Amriki when ISIS supporters began circulating news of his death on Twitter in May 2016.[2] He had been killed with his wife—Umm Isa al-Amriki—in an airstrike on his home in northern Syria. Both were prominent online recruiters for ISIS, using Twitter and the encrypted messaging service Telegram to encourage supporters to migrate to ISIS-controlled territory in Syria, Iraq, and Libya.

Umm Isa al-Amriki's first Telegram post, created on January 15, 2016, announced:

> This channel is dedicated to everyone who wishes to do Hijrah [migration] to the blessed land of Sham [Syria].
>
> I condemn all acts of peaceful coexistence between Muslims and non-Muslims and strongly condemn every coconut [false] Muslim who abides in Dar Al-Kufr [land of disbelief].
>
> I will be posting daily reminders, pictures of Sham, short articles and general information about my life here in Sham.
>
> I can be contacted on @snowwhitewidorio (strictly sisters only)
>
> I am a married sister so all brothers will be directed to the Beast who married me on his telegram (@honeyNtea).
>
> May Allaah grant us all martyrdom in His path and enable us to cause terror in the hearts and minds of all those who fight against the Caliphate, ameen.

Umm Isa al-Amriki's channel was just like every other female pro-ISIS account. It was full of ball-achingly boring "reminders" about the dangers of the "dunya" [the material world]. It was obsessed with female modesty, and the right and wrong ways to protect it. It was hectoring and violent: "Who out there will get up and kill the kuffars in the west?," Umm Isa al-Amriki asked her "brothers" back home, taking them to task for their lack of manly honor. Now and again she would shine a crack of light onto her private life, posting pictures of evening meals, a stash of cheap chocolate, and her gun collection. Like many ISIS sisters on social media, she engaged in a lot of tough talk about wanting to die. In one post, dated January 18, 2016, she declared:

> Alhamdulillah ['thanks and Praise to God'] finally got my Hizam [suicide belt] today. May Allah subhana wa ta'ala ['glory be to God'] grant me the opportunity to use it soon, to grant me the honor to sacrifice my self for Him, for His deen [religion] (to kill the kuffars). May Allah subhana wa ta'ala grant us all shahadah [martyrdom] Ameen.

About her husband, Abu Isa al-Amriki, Umm Isa al-Amriki said little. Her last post, in which she advised, "Always remember, u were created with a greater purpose & for a greater place -not to fret over this world & to carry it's worries with u," is dated April 19, 2016. She was reportedly killed three days later with Abu Isa al-Amriki. According to the then Pentagon Press Secretary Peter Cook:

> I want to note that on April 22 [2016] coalition forces conducted an airstrike targeting Sudanese national Abu Sa'ad al-Sudani, also known as Abu Isa Al Amriki, an ISIL external attack planner. This strike happened near Al-Bab, Syria. We can now confirm that al-Sudani and his wife, Shadi Jabar Khalil Mohammad, also known as Umm Isa Amriki, an Australian national were both killed in this airstrike. Al-Sudani was involved in planning attacks against the United States, Canada and the United Kingdom. Both al-Sudani and his wife were active in recruiting foreign fighters in efforts to inspire attacks against Western interests. The death of al-Sudani and Shadi remove influential ISIL recruiters and extremists who actively sought to harm Western interests and further disrupts and degrades ISIL's ability to plot external attacks.[3]

This was revealing in several respects—and not just because the Pentagon was still doggedly sticking with the acronym "ISIL."[4] It was the first time a public official had revealed the identity of Umm Isa al-Amriki: a 20-year-old Australian woman named Shadi Jabar Khalil Mohammad.[5] This woman's brother, a 15-year-old named Farhad, had shot dead a police civil servant outside the New South Wales Police headquarters in Parramatta, Australia, on October 2, 2015. He was killed soon after in a gunfight with officers outside the police headquarters. A day before the attack Shadi, according to her parents, had gone missing: she had taken a Singapore Airlines flight to Istanbul, where she boarded a bus to the Syria border.[6]

Cook's statement was also revealing because it confirmed that Abu Sa'ad al-Sudani and Abu Isa al-Amriki were one and the same person. In addition to this, the statement claimed that Abu Isa al-Amriki/Abu Sa'ad al-Sudani (henceforth al-Amriki) was a Sudanese national, which surprised many ISIS experts who up to that point were working on the assumption, based on his *kunya*, that he was an American.

As Cook's statement suggests, al-Amriki was far more than just a brash online recruiter of jihadi talent; he was also a prominent "external attack planner"—i.e., he was active in plotting terrorist attacks on targets in the West, using encrypted messaging devices to inspire and operationally guide his willing distant acolytes. In a report on "How ISIS Guides World's Terror Plots from Afar," published nine months after the Pentagon's press statement, *The New York Times* journalist Rukmini Callimachi described how al-Amriki had played a leading role in "grooming attackers" in India, Canada, and Britain, "as well as at least three other young men in suburbs across America."[7] One of these men was Aaron Travis Daniels, a 20-year-old warehouse worker from Columbus, Ohio.[8]

Daniels, who was being watched by the FBI Joint Terrorism Task Force since September 2015, wired $250 to al-Amriki via an intermediary in January 2016.[9] He had also communicated to al-Amriki his desire to travel to the caliphate in Syria.

Prior to hearing about Daniels, I hadn't paid much attention to al-Amriki. But in reading the Department of Justice's press release announcing Daniels's arrest on November 7, 2016, I was struck by one detail in particular: al-Amriki had advised Daniels to travel to Libya via Trinidad.[10] Daniels had relayed this to an undercover FBI agent, telling him that he had planned to go to Libya via Trinidad so "the kuffar [non-believers] don't track me."[11] It wasn't the destination that caught my interest; by the close of 2015, when Daniels had first reached out to al-Amriki via Telegram, ISIS recruiters were urging would-be recruits either to stay put in their home countries and conduct attacks there or to make their way to other ISIS provinces, like Libya, that were easier to reach. What startled me, rather, was the route: how did al-Amriki know that Trinidad was such a soft touch for jihadi travelers? And who did al-Amriki know in Trinidad who could assist Daniels if he needed to stay on the island for a few days prior to commencing his travel to Libya? It then quickly dawned on me that Stuart Mohamed, who was one of the first Trinis to go to Syria, was known by the *kunya* Abu Isa. This is from Shane Crawford's interview in *Dabiq*, published in the last installment of that magazine in July 2016:

> I, along with my brothers in Islam Abu 'Abdillah (another convert from Christianity), Abu 'Isa, and a number of other brothers from Trinidad that later made hijrah [migration] after us formed a group and would deal with some of the issues of the Muslims that people were afraid to deal with.[12]

This was the core of the cell that Peter had mentioned: a quasi-paramilitary group that traded in guns and sharia implementation in Chaguanas, Rio Claro, and Diego Martin. "Whenever the disbelievers in Trinidad would kill or harm a Muslim," Crawford explained, "we would take revenge. We would work to accumulate money in order to buy weapons and ammo. Alhamdulillah ['thanks and Praise to God'], we were successful in many operations, and this was only by Allah's grace."[13] One such "operation" was the murder of Joel Malchan and Dharmendra Sookdeo in retaliation for the killing of Ishmael Baksh, a Rio Claro resident and a member of Crawford's cell. Crawford not only described in *Dabiq* how this murder went down; he also implicated himself, Abu 'Abdillah, and Abu 'Isa in the murder. "Following the operation," he said, "Abu 'Abdillah and Abu 'Isa were arrested, and I went into hiding."[14] "Once more," he continued, "Allah bestowed a tremendous favor on us as Abu 'Isa was released pending investigation. Abu 'Abdillah was also released and we left Trinidad one-by-one."[15]

Later on in the interview, Crawford mentions Abu 'Isa again, referring to his "martyrdom" in "Marista, a village close to Azaz, during the height of the Sahwah [uprising] in the Levant." According to Crawford:

> While he was stationed in ribat [military base] in the village, the apostates came and attacked with a large force, including BMPs [tanks] and heavy weapons. The brothers were about 15 in number and were only armed with Kalashnikovs. After the initial skirmish, the brothers decided to withdraw. Abu 'Isa and another brother stayed

back to cover them as the others withdrew. When they were looking to make their exit they were flanked by the apostates and Abu 'Isa was shot several times, but he didn't die until the apostates approached and executed him with a close range head shot as he was lying on the ground wounded. Alhamdulillah ['thanks and Praise to God'], later on that day the brothers took back the village, and they later mentioned to us that when they buried Abu 'Isa and the other martyrs, there was a very strong smell of musk.[16]

Given that Crawford's interview was accompanied by a picture of five Trinis, with the words "Abu 'Abdillah (center)" written beneath it, it wasn't difficult to identify him: Abu 'Abdillah is Milton Algernon (AKA Fareed Mustapha). The other Trinis in the photo are Chris Lewis, Anthony Hamlet (AKA Faisal Farooq), Aleem Alexander, and a Afro-Trini I haven't yet been able to identify. The process of identifying Abu 'Isa was more protracted, but it wasn't difficult. I contacted my friend Mark Bassant, a multi-media journalist who works for a national TV station in Trinidad, to see if he knew any details about the double murder that Crawford described in *Dabiq*. He told me that it had taken place in Chaguanas, and that Crawford, Algernon, and an East Indian man named Stuart Mohamed were the muscle who pulled it off. Stuart, he said, was the getaway driver. He also sent me a link to a *T&T Newsday* article, dated December 3, 2013: Titled "Man in court for a bullet," its subheading read in bold, "FREEPORT resident Stuart Mohammed yesterday appeared before a Couva magistrate charged for possession of a round of ammunition."[17] According to Bassant, Crawford and Algernon had fled the car just before Stuart was stopped and searched at a police road-block, whereupon officers found a bullet in his car. The *T&T Newsday* article noted that Stuart had been arrested on November 24, the day of the Chaguanas hit,[18] in connection with a capital offense, and that he had been granted bail on November 29, 2013.[19] It also reported that the case was adjourned to December 27, 2013, by which point Mohamed was in Syria, having traveled first to Venezuela, where he met up with Crawford and Algernon. Stuart's role in the Chaguanas hit was later confirmed to me by one of the arresting officers, who also relayed that he knew Stuart had skipped bail and gone to Syria. "Our info was that he was killed in Syria," he added. About a year after Stuart had fled Trinidad, his mugshot turned up on the Facebook page of a local law and order TV show called "Beyond The Tape."[20] To the right of the mugshot, in which Stuart looks every bit the hardcore jihadi, with his long black beard and scowl, is written, in capitals, his full name—STUART RAFFICK MOHAMED—and the crime for which he is wanted: POSSESSION OF AMMUNITION. His last known address is listed as Mission Road, Freeport. "RIP he died in Syria," someone commented below the post on February 22, 2017.

There can be no doubt, then, that Abu 'Isa was Stuart, but was Stuart al-Amriki? I contacted Stuart's older brother and mother to see if they would talk to me about Stuart, and confirm when he died. But they didn't respond to my emails. I spoke with two of Stuart's old hiking buddies, but they were reluctant to say very much about him, other than what I already knew (that he had "done something very bad in Trinidad," as one of them put it, and gone to Syria and was killed there). After many months of probing, I finally found an associate of Stuart's who was willing to speak to me about him. He said that Stuart's full *kunya* was Abu Isa al-Amriki and that he was killed in Syria, although he didn't know when. And he confirmed Stuart's role in the double murder in Chaguanas. But why did Stuart use the *kunya* "al-Amriki," which means "the American" in Arabic? The associate told me that many Trinis who joined ISIS had some connection to the United States and that, in any case, it was common for them to use "al-Amriki" on account of Trinidad being so close to South America. Sean Parson, for example, took on the *kunya* Abu Khalid al-Amriki and he was as Trini as *aloo pie*. The associate also conjectured that the affiliation with America gave Trinis an added kudos among Arabs and Middle Easterners who prized defectors from America and had never heard of Trinidad.

But why Abu 'Isa? In Arabic "Abu" means "father of," and in Islam it is common practice for fighters to use the name of their eldest son in their *kunya*. Stuart, I learned from his Facebook Page, had two sons. On October 30, 2014, when he would have been in Syria for ten months, he posted a photo of them. One looks no more than 2 years old, while the other must be around 5. Stuart, who is smiling and wearing a white *shalwar kameez*, is holding the younger boy with his right arm. With his other hand, he is patting the head of the older boy standing alongside him. The photo was taken in Trinidad. Below it are four comments:

> [**Stuart Mohamed's sister**] Cute baby what's his name
> **Stuart Mohamed** Come on sis what kind of aunty you will be if you don't even know your nephew's name.
> **Stuart Mohamed** In case you forgot his name is Sa'ad
> **Stuart Mohamed** and please don't forget his brother's name ISA

This seemed like more than just a coincidence: Al-Amriki used not just one *kunya* but two, and the second one was Abu Sa'ad al Sudani. Quite why Stuart would choose "Sudani" as his geo-tag is a mystery, but Sa'ad is the name of Stuart's youngest son.

Around the same time I made this discovery I acquired a recording of al-Amriki from a British journalist who had tried to entrap him. It's a two-minute voice-note that al-Amriki sent via his Telegram account. In it he encourages the journalist, who is posing as an ISIS supporter from the UK, to send money, computer equipment, and cell phones to "Sham" [Syria].[21] When I played the recording to the Trini criminologist and jihadist expert Daurius Figueira, he was categorical:

> **Figueira:** Classic Trini Indian—Muslim. Two of the idioms he used—classic Trini Indian.
> **Cottee:** The way he said 'As-Salaam-Alaikum' ['Peace be unto you'], that sounds Trini Indian to you?
> **Figueira:** That is Trini Indian Muslim—'As-Salaam-Alaikum', because their dialect is different from ours [Afro-Trinis], their dialect was formed on an Urdu-Hindi base down there [south Trinidad], they speak entirely different to us…and the way he is speaking the English, that is the way they speak when they leave here—Trini Indian Muslim—they go to Arabia, they get exposed to Arabic in their daily life, and they learn the Arabic, that is the kind of English they come back talking…I fed up listening to them talking English so…That a Trini, that a Trini Indian Muslim.

**Cottee:** Yeah, he doesn't sound like an ordinary Trini.

**Figueira:** No, they don't talk corridor Indian, and you have African Muslims in Trinidad who live in central and who went to Medina [in Saudi Arabia] and come back and they be on Channel 8 preaching and you hear the same English…That a special English that they've developed and want to show everybody that they are Quranic-Arabic literate…A Trini Indian Muslim…That is he. That is a Trini Indian Muslim, a Trini Indian Muslim… And that is one who is projecting the imagery of a cleric, a sheikh… he playing sheikh.

Two other sources—both cops—were also adamant that the voice on the recording was that of an East Indian Trini.

According to Crawford's *Dabiq* interview, Stuart was killed in combat in a village near Azaz, "during the height of the Sahwah [uprising] in the Levant." Crawford doesn't put a date on his death, but Azaz is a city roughly 20 miles northwest of Aleppo in northwestern Syria. Recall that the Pentagon confirmed that al-Amriki, too, was killed in the Aleppo province (in Al-Bab). Yet Crawford's account makes it clear that Stuart was killed in combat, while the Pentagon says that al-Amriki was killed in an airstrike by the anti-ISIS coalition. Both accounts must be treated with some degree of skepticism, given the propagandistic purposes to which they can be put by both sides. What is certain is that Stuart was still alive as late as September 1, 2015, when he uploaded his last Facebook post. He was also, according to a police file I saw on Stuart following his arrest on November 24, 2013, 5'8" tall and thick-set, weighing 190 pounds: big enough to warrant the moniker "the Beast."

"His family are millionaires," Peter, the ex-spook, said, referring to Stuart, who used to work as an IT manager in the family-owned business—a packaging company called R&C Enterprises based in Freeport, Chaguanas. "He a born Muslim," he added. And he was on Peter's radar for a long time—since at least 2003, when Stuart would have just graduated from UWI. According to Peter, "Stuart was always searching for something," and that search led him to Nazim Mohammed and his mosque in Rio Claro. As Peter describes him, Stuart was a true believer—and very radical: "He was opposed to the whole western system." At some point—Peter didn't say when—Stuart split from his wife, who didn't share his religious fervor, and moved away from the family home in Freeport and went to live closer to Nazim in Rio Claro. Peter also told me that at one point Stuart, Crawford, Algernon, and several others had all come under Ashmead Choate's influence, but Choate, evidently, was a difficult and divisive figure, so they broke with him and "ended up pledging *bay'ah* [allegiance] to Nazim." Choate, Peter said, went to Iraq to become a jurist for ISIS, but was executed by the group. This wasn't the first time I'd heard this story about Choate: that he was killed by ISIS because he fell out with senior emirs on matters of jurisprudence. Crawford's *Dabiq* interview, however, contradicts this: Choate, he said, was killed in battle in the Iraqi city of Ramadi.[22] Crawford described Choate as "a man of sound knowledge," but no one I'd spoken to in Trinidad (except Umar Abdullah) had a good word to say about him. According to Peter, Stuart thought "he was shit-town," which in Trinidad is a way of saying that he didn't rate him very highly.

\*\*\*

Is Stuart Mohamed and Abu Isa al-Amriki one and the same person? The weight of the evidence certainly points to this, but in the absence of any official confirmation from the T&T security services, and given that the Pentagon identified al-Amriki as Sudanese, it must remain an open question. What is certain is that Stuart should never have been allowed to leave Trinidad to take up arms, either as a fighter or as a "virtual planner," for ISIS. After the High Court granted him bail on November 29, 2013, Stuart was ordered by a Senior Magistrate to surrender his passport to the police, since state prosecutors deemed him to be a flight risk.[23] But within days of being granted bail he walked out of Trinidad's Piarco airport with the tranquility of a man who knew he was untouchable. One anonymous security source told me that there is no record that Stuart traveled with his passport and that he likely paid a counterfeiter to acquire a false one. False passports are not hard to come by in Trinidad, he said. Soon after, scores of other Trinis followed Stuart, encountering little or no resistance from T&T's security apparatus.

One woman, who, like Stuart, was on the radar of the security services, having been detained in Venezuela with twenty-one other Trinis in March 2014 on suspicion of traveling to join ISIS in Syria,[24] was also able to travel unhindered to Syria, with her four young children, within a year of her detention in Caracas.[25] Many other Trinis, and some with extensive rap-sheets, were allowed to do the same.

This was not because security officials didn't know who these people were or what they were planning. On the contrary, it was because of a policy of non-intervention on the part of the government at that time. Gary Griffith, who served as Minister of National Security between September 2013 and February 2015, told me that his "concern as Minster of National Security was not them [fighters from T&T] going across—they were free to go across, if they wanted—my concern was to ensure that they do not come back." Griffith's honesty in admitting this impressed me, and given the heat associated with so many of those who had fled the country to join ISIS, I could understand why the government was happy to see the back of them. But even as he said it I was taken aback by the short-sightedness of this approach. As well as exhibiting an indifference toward the citizens of Iraq and Syria, against whom the Trini ISIS mujahideen would soon be waging holy war, it showed a disregard for the welfare of the Trini children who were, in effect, trafficked to Syria and Iraq. The Trini ISIS mujahideen may have been, to quote Griffith, "free to go across," but they shouldn't have been at liberty to take their children with them, not only because it was a warzone, but also because, once in Syria or Iraq, some of the boys, barely into their teens, would have been conscripted into ISIS as combatants or suicide bombers on the frontlines, while the teenaged girls would have been married off to ISIS fighters.

It wasn't until 2016 that the T&T government's attitude toward ISIS started to shift. In September of that year, just as foreign fighter travel to Syria had all but dried up,[26] the government designated ISIS as a terrorist organization,[27] and in February 2017 it tabled new legislative proposals designed to hinder travel to jihadi hot spots abroad and to clamp down on terrorist financing.[28] But it was all too little and too late, given that so many Trinis had already gone to join the caliphate and that ISIS was now on the back-foot and struggling to hold on to its territory.

The proposals were eventually passed in August 2018,[29] but not without a great deal of opposition.[30] One sticking point—and there were many—was a suggestion to criminalize the glorification of terrorism. In April 2018 Susan Francois, director of the Financial Intelligence Unit, explained to the Parliamentary Select Committee on the Anti-Terrorism Amendment Bill that, while the proposal could be seen as "contentious," it was designed to stop people from praising or celebrating acts of terrorism in such a way as to encourage others to commit further terrorist atrocities. Committee chairman and Attorney General Faris Al-Rawi, though supportive of the proposal in principle, expressed his concerns that, since Trinis have a "dynamic and peculiar form of humour and public commentary," they may be unfairly targeted by any such provision. "We say unacceptable things that are intended to mean otherwise. We are Trinis and there must be a careful approach," he said.[31] This particular proposal was subsequently dropped.[32]

If there was an attitude of tolerance on the part of the T&T government toward ISIS recruitment in the country at the high water mark of the caliphate in Syria and Iraq, there was a conspiracy of silence within the communities most affected by jihadist radicalization in the country. Many didn't want to speak out against ISIS, not because they were sympathetic to its worldview, although many undoubtedly were, but because they didn't want to draw negative attention to Muslims in T&T, nor give the authorities a license to interfere in their communities. Most of all, they didn't want to be seen as "native informants" or "sell outs."

And not a few Muslims in Trinidad simply followed the example of that large African bird which, when in grave danger, chooses to bury its head in the sand. Consider, for example, Fuad Abu Bakr's cognitive dissonance on the question of ISIS. When I asked him about the group, he told me, firmly, "Who is ISIS? I don't know who that is. Honestly, it's all bullshit and media ... I don't know if [Abu Bakr] Al-Baghdadi exists, I don't know if [Abu Musab] al-Zarqawi exists, I don't know if [Osama] bin Laden even exists ... I know how news is made." Yet, at the same time, Fuad wasn't exactly short of ideas about why so many Trinis had gone to Syria and Iraq to fight for ISIS. Nor did he exactly deny knowledge of who was going from Trinidad: "They're good guys, they're nice people ... Their faith is strong enough. They're convinced that it's the right thing that they're doing."

Or consider former PNM deputy political leader and attorney Nafeesa Mohammed's lamentable efforts to defend a young girl for wearing a black hoodie with the ISIS flag emblazoned on it. And this was no ordinary teenager playing for laughs: the girl in question was the daughter of Chinonesu Luqman, a convicted extremist who also happened to be Shane Crawford's brother-in-law and a fellow detainee in the 2011 state of emergency. And she wore it in full public view at Piarco International Airport on the very day that her father returned to Trinidad after serving a two-and-a-half-year prison sentence for espionage in Venezuela (he was one of the twenty-two Trinis detained in that country in 2014 on suspicion of traveling to join ISIS in Syria[33]). Quite what she was thinking is anyone's guess. But even more baffling was Nafeesa Mohammed's response to the incident. Just "because something has Arabic sayings on it, [doesn't mean] it's ISIS or it's evil,"[34] she told the *T&T Guardian*. Which would have been perfectly fine had the hooded top in question not borne the distinct and unmistakable iconography of ISIS. Keen to change the subject, she said: "If you have such sayings on a jersey or jacket, it doesn't mean you follow ISIS. But some sentiments are now giving rise to Islamophobia, stigmatising everything that is Islam and misconstruing its nature. I hope people would be aware and understand we must respect each others' beliefs." The bit about respecting others' beliefs was a laudable sentiment, and Mohammed was no doubt right to warn against the menace of anti-Muslim bigotry. But it wasn't clear what any of this had to do with calling out Luqman's daughter for wearing a hoodie bearing the ISIS flag. And, of course, if anyone was to be called out for "stigmatizing" Islam, it was clearly Luqman's daughter for covering herself in the symbolism of a group that the vast majority of Muslims reject as unIslamic.

But as feeble as Nafeesa Mohammed's apologetics were, they were wholly in keeping with a broader discourse that was in almost total denial about ISIS and Islamist radicalization in Trinidad at that time.

Even as late as December 2018, when Trinidad's status as a hotbed of ISIS recruitment was scarcely in doubt and the subject of many perplexed international news stories and video documentaries,[35] the Attorney General, Faris Al-Rawi, was adamant that the country didn't have a violent extremism problem. "The number may look larger than somewhere else," he told the British *Guardian*, "but I don't accept for one moment that we have a problem that is much larger than anywhere else," adding, "I don't think that we are any more vulnerable than any other country is."[36] In the very same article Yasin Abu Bakr was paraphrased as saying, "European nations had no moral grounds to criticise ISIS beheadings, because of the use of the guillotine during the French revolution."[37] Presumably, Bakr himself was not so compromised, but it was revealing and utterly predictable that he, just like his son Fuad, couldn't scrap together a clear-eyed condemnation of ISIS's barbarity, preferring instead to single out the supposed hypocrisy of European countries.

\*\*\*

On May 26, 2017, Rodney Charles, the United National Congress (UNC) Member of Parliament for Naparima, a town in southwest Trinidad, stood up from his seat in the House of Representatives, T&T's national parliament, and voiced his concerns about what he called the "rising crime epidemic" in the country.[38] After reeling off a list of recent high-profile robberies, kidnappings, and murders, he condemned the

PNM government of Prime Minister Keith Rowley for, in his eyes, failing to address the rising tide of crime. "We are in the top 10," he said, referring to a report on the countries with the highest murder rates in the world.[39] "But it gets worse than that, Mr. Deputy Speaker," Charles continued.[40] "When it comes to terrorism, the whole world *washin dey mout* [bad talking] on Trinidad and Tobago. Let me say 'mouth'. Speak with elegance—'mouth.'"[41] Charles was referring to a recent spate of articles on ISIS recruitment in Trinidad, including one that I had written for *The Atlantic*,[42] which he cited, quoting the statistic that Trinidad had the highest per capita rate of ISIS recruits in the Western hemisphere. "We have people outside of Trinidad and Tobago who know more about—call names, dates, time, events, plane tickets—know more [than us] about terrorism in Trinidad," he lamented.[43] Charles then engaged in *washin he own mout* on the Minister of National Security Edmund Dillon, whom he quoted as saying that ISIS poses "no threat to T&T right now."[44] What, Charles wanted to know, was the government doing about the crime problem as well as the threat of ISIS-sponsored terrorism? Responding, Dillon deflected and changed the subject to crime and corruption under the previous government of the People's Partnership Coalition (PPC), of which the UNC was the largest party. He also reminded Charles that most of the Trinis who left to join ISIS had done so during the previous government's time in power.[45] What he didn't address, however, was how the government was now taking seriously the threat of terrorism. This did not go unnoticed by Dr. Roodal Moonilal, UNC Member of Parliament for Oropouche East, a constituency in the southwest of the country, just below San Fernando. "As soon as we left office," Moonilal said, referring to the PPC, "we warned this Government ... that we have had persons leaving and going to foreign lands to be radicalized and it posed the single most critical element of a threat to this country."[46] He then alluded to the attempted coup of 1990, warning the government that "if you do not get your act together and deal seriously with these matters there may be another attempt of overthrow the State."[47] Referring to the Manchester

Arena terrorist attack in 2017, he said, "Do not believe that what happened at the Manchester Arena can only happen in Manchester and cannot happen here."[48]

Moonilal had expressed the same concerns to me when I interviewed him in the summer of 2016. Speaking over a lunch in the Hyatt, in Port of Spain, he told me that, in his view, Islamist extremism was "the biggest security challenge of this generation." A few months earlier he had claimed in parliament that over 400 Trinis had left the country to join ISIS in Syria and Iraq.[49] I pressed him on this: where did he get that number from? It sounded like an exaggeration to me—maybe 300–350 at the high end, but over 400? "Whether it's 80 or 400 is a moot point, it's the same challenge," he said, clarifying that the 400 figure included children; official estimates, apparently, did not. The data he was quoting from, he told me, was given to him by "a whistleblower" from inside the T&T intelligence apparatus. This consists of two agencies: the Strategic Services Agency (SSA), whose remit includes all serious crimes,[50] and Special Branch, the intelligence unit of the T&T Police Service (TTPS). Moonilal didn't say which agency the whistleblower worked for. But he had plenty to say about the government's lax approach to the threat of international terrorism. "My concern," he said, "wasn't an argument over numbers, but over policy. What are you [the government] doing about these persons who have gone to Syria and do you allow them to come back here to Trinidad and create a Caribbean epicenter for terrorism?" "Could you deny them citizenship and entry into T&T?," he asked, addressing a debate that has taken on a grave urgency now that the ISIS caliphate has collapsed and thousands of captured foreign fighters are stranded in detention camps in Syria. He expressed his disbelief that "to this day [August 2016] ISIS is not proscribed in T&T, meaning that you can go and train with ISIS for 2–3 years and come back here with all the rights and privileges of a citizen of T&T." But this was also true in 2014 and 2015, when Moonilal's own party was in power.

Between 2016 and 2018 the PNM government's official positon was that Trinis who went to Syria and Iraq would not be stripped of their citizenship and were free to return, where they would be closely monitored and placed on a de-radicalization program, the details of which have never been made known.[51] Moonilal dismissed this as "weak and feeble." "They should be denied statehood," he said of those who had left. He also doubted the state's ability to track returnees, should they find their way back to T&T. "This is a country where you have a murder every 18 hours, where you have people walking around with hand-grenades in a bag as if it's mangoes." This was a reference to an incident in May 2016, where a man fleeing the police mistakenly dropped a hand-grenade from the bag he was carrying.[52] "If you cannot keep an eye on a man walking about with a bag of hand-grenades," he said, "can you really keep an eye on someone coming back from Syria?" Moonilal then outlined his case for the creation of a specialized, anti-terrorism unit within the national security setup. Currently there isn't one, and the burden of monitoring terrorist-related activity is shared by both the SSA and the Special Branch, two agencies which do not always collaborate seamlessly. ("There are challenges," a senior member of the SSA told me about the relationship, without elaborating.) As the interview drew to a close Moonilal said that he would see about getting me a photocopy of the whistleblower's file, but I never did get to see it, despite making repeated requests to have his secretary make it available to me. As I walked toward Port of Spain's City Gate in search of a *Maxi*, the thought occurred to me that I could probably pick up a hand-grenade in Chaguanas for around the same price as a mango in the Hyatt.

***

Gary Griffith is currently the Commissioner of the TTPS.[53] Since taking up that role in August 2018 he has redefined what it means to be a Police Commissioner in the county. While his predecessors were risk-averse bureaucrats and desk-men, turning up to press conferences only when they had to, Griffith is a man of action who convenes a press conference every time he leaves the office—or so it can seem. On his first day on the job, he told the press,

> I am here to serve my God, my country and the citizens of this great country. As I stated before there will be no honeymoon period and I do not expect any. This is not going to be the Gary Griffith show. I intend to work as hard as possible with all the relevant stakeholders to ensure that the most fundamental rights of citizens of this country are protected.[54]

Since then, *The Gary Griffith Show* airs most days and evenings on the TV news in T&T (I am being ironic here, dear reader: no such show by that name runs in T&T). In many of these appearances the star of the show is wearing not a beige khaki uniform—the standard apparel of the Police Commissioner—but a blue tactical suit worn by patrol officers. When questioned about this, Griffith told *T&T Newsday*, "I intend to dress and to be on the ground with my troops. And how my troops will dress, I will dress in the appropriate manner."[55] Griffith, clearly, likes military-style uniforms, and has spent much of his adult life wearing one: before going into politics and the law-and-order business, he was a highly decorated captain in the army. By early 2019 Griffith had added a new edition to his wardrobe: a camouflage outfit with matching cap. This occasioned much critical discussion in T&T,[56] as well as a few off-color jokes about what Griffith wears at night in the bedroom. Griffith's critics were concerned about the creeping militarization of policing in the country, while the jokers were worried about the creeping militarization of the commissioner's love-life.

Tom Zoellner, an American journalist who wrote a superb piece on the murder of Prosecutor Dana Seetahal, described Griffith as "bluster prone."[57] This is probably a bit harsh, but it isn't without foundation. Griffith likes to talk, and often his talk is fast and big. When I interviewed him about Trini foreign fighters in February 2016 he was vehement and detailed in his criticism of the government's lack of preparedness in dealing with the issue. About the prospect of trained ISIS militants returning to Trinidad with their radicalized families, he was emphatic: "They should not be allowed re-entry … If they know that it's a one-way ticket to hell, that is the ultimate deterrent." "It is unfortunate," he added, "that the new Minister of National Security [Edmund Dillon] made a statement saying that if they are citizens it is their right to return if they want. I think that is flawed." Griffith's fear is that returning foreign fighters will plot attacks in T&T, as well as try to radicalize others to the jihadi cause.

He also expressed frustration that his own proposal to create what he called "a counter-terrorism intelligence unit" for monitoring terrorist threats, introduced when he was Minister of National Security, was blocked by the current government. "We must have a unit which deals specifically with terrorist activity," he insisted, a view that Moonilal also holds. And he poured scorn over Dillon's "unfortunate" comment that ISIS poses "no threat to T&T"—a gift, it seems, that keeps on giving for opposition Members of Parliament. Dillon, he said, has "a good heart and means well." But "he's burying his head in the sand. He thinks God is a Trini." Dillon did not respond to my numerous requests for comment.

***

On Thursday, February 8, 2018, just days before Carnival, the TTPS held an "emergency media conference" in Port of Spain, announcing that four people had been detained for questioning "in relation to a threat to Carnival 2018 celebrations." Michael Jackman, the T&T police official who delivered the announcement, didn't and wouldn't elaborate on what the threat was, saying only that it was criminal in nature and that it had been "neutralized." TV6 journalist Mark Bassant asked Jackman if he could confirm whether the threat involved a planned attack on the US Embassy on either Carnival Monday or Tuesday. Jackman could not: "What I can say at this time is that four persons are presently detained and are being interviewed by members of the Trinidad and Tobago Police Service."[58]

A day after the press conference, CNN ran a story on how the US military helped "thwart Trinidad carnival terror attack."[59] The authors of the piece, Ryan Browne and Barbara Starr, wrote that "US military personnel from US Southern Command, which oversees US military operations in the region, advised and assisted local Trinidadian security forces in apprehending the four extremists who are believed to be part of a network engaged in plotting terror attacks."[60] "Trinidad and Tobago," they pointed out, "has long been an area of concern for the US military and intelligence communities as it is assessed to be home to ISIS sympathizers."[61] In the days following the TTPS press conference the police conducted searches at the Nur-E-Islam Masjid in San Juan, as well as at several private residences nearby. (Shazam Mohammed, who was an associate of Zaid Abdul Hamid, was a member of the Nur-E-Islam Masjid prior to leaving for Syria to join ISIS.) The police also brought in a further eleven suspects for questioning. By February 16, just over a week after the TTPS press conference, all had been released, except for two, who were jointly charged with possession of a firearm. All of the suspects were Muslims.[62]

When I first saw the CNN story I remember thinking that something seemed off about it. Why would the government announce that it had foiled a plot to attack Carnival right before the event itself? Wouldn't that cause panic among the would-be attendees? And what if there were plotters who the police didn't know about? Wouldn't publicly announcing the plot risk activating them? In the event Carnival passed without incident, other than the usual robberies, knifings, and murders.[63] But there was no terrorist attack, and all of the detainees, bar two, were released without charge. An editorial in the *T&T Guardian* described this as an "egg on face moment" for the police and government,[64] who had announced with such fanfare just a week before how it had thwarted a terrorist plot on that most sacred of all things in T&T, namely its annual Carnival, an event that brings in around US $50 million each year.[65]

So, then, if there really was a plot to launch a terrorist attack during or directly on Carnival why was no one charged on terrorism-related offenses? And why was the government so keen to publicize the foiling of the so-called plot? One possibility is that there was *no* plot, and that the whole thing was a public relations stunt designed to make the government look like it was finally taking seriously the threat of terrorism and pro-actively responding to it. A second possibility is that there was a plot, but that it wasn't sufficiently developed for any charges to be made to stick; perhaps the police had come under pressure to act so that the government could publicly announce a success in the war on terrorism just in time for Carnival, when much of the world—well, certainly the United States and Britain—would be watching.

Both possibilities seem plausible. What cannot be doubted, however, is that the government needed to change the optics and show its allies, especially the Americans and the British, that it was serious about terrorism and on the front-foot.

Almost exactly a year before Carnival 2018, on February 19, 2017, President Donald Trump telephoned Prime Minister Rowley. This wasn't a call about real estate and the potential for a future golf course in the Caribbean; this was a call about the threat of international terrorism and transitional organized crime.[66] No doubt Trump would have wanted Rowley's assurance that he had a handle on both matters. Just two days after that call *The New York Times* published an in-depth story titled, "Trying to Stanch Trinidad's Flow of Young Recruits to ISIS."[67] It noted: "American officials worry about having a breeding ground for extremists so close to the United States, fearing that Trinidadian fighters could return from the Middle East and attack American diplomatic and oil installations in Trinidad, or even take a three-and-a-half-hour flight to Miami." This report would have added further pressure on Rowley's government, as would have the travel advisory issued in October 2017 by the British Foreign and Commonwealth Office warning, "Terrorists are likely to try to carry out attacks in Trinidad & Tobago. Attacks could be indiscriminate, including in places visited by foreigners."[68] Of course, none of this is to suggest that the Carnival plot was fabricated, but the zeal with which the government publicized its foiling suggests that it was particularly keen to signal to an international audience that it was firmly on top of its terrorism problem.

On February 14, 2018, a day after the last day of Carnival, Prime Minister Rowley held a press conference in which he insisted that the Carnival plot was "no joke." "I do not know that we have faced this level of activity before," he said, adding, "We do have Anti-Terrorism legislation in the Parliament and all of this will strengthen our ability to deal with it."[69] Obviously wounded by suspicions that the plot was fabricated, Rowley then doubled down by saying, in Parliament, that it was "common knowledge" that there were pro-ISIS groups in T&T and that "the monitoring of such persons is an integral part of our national security."[70]

"Yes," he flatly said, in response to an Opposition MP's question as to whether "there was anything in Trinidad and Tobago that could be considered an ISIS cell or satellite."[71] Just two days later the Attorney General Faris Al-Rawi sought to backtrack on this admission. The Prime Minister, he told *T&T Newsday*, "didn't specifically state there is quote unquote, confirmed ISIS cells here."[72] Perhaps Al-Rawi didn't want to overstate the nature of the terrorist threat in T&T. Or perhaps he was trying to forestall the criticism that his government had been sleeping on that threat by allowing an ISIS cell to operate under its watch. Regardless, this confusion or ambiguity was emblematic of a deeper malaise within the government about the growth and threat of violent extremism in the country.

# 6

# The Lost Generation

*I want my kids back…[They're] innocent. They don't know nothing about terrorists, terrorism or guns. This is not part of my life and I don't want it to be part of their life.*
Marvin Roach, December 8, 2014[1]

*I just want to be normal and go back to a normal society, sleep in a nice bed, eat nice food, watch TV and laugh.*
Gailon Su, March 29, 2019[2]

*Soooooo….. you went to do your SHIT overseas get your ass in jail and now you want the state with our facking money to bail your ass out and bring you back steuppps*
Patrick Lewis, Facebook Comment Post, November 26, 2018

On January 9, 2019, the Kurdish People's Protection Units, or YPG, issued a statement reporting that they had captured eight foreign fighters in the town of Hajin in eastern Syria, where the last remnants of ISIS were holed up, including a 16-year-old American named Soulay Noah Su (AKA Abu Souleiman al-Amriki).[3] The YPG also released a poster with mugshots of all eight captives.

Soulay Noah Su stands out like the proverbial sore thumb, and not just because he is the only black face among the motley crew of jihadists. The Uzbeki to Su's right looks like he's been holed up not in a besieged town, but in an actual hole. His beard is gray, long, and disheveled, and his eyes look sunken and depleted. The other men, all much older than Su, look like they've just returned from a month-long bender in some dank eastern-European city. Su, by contrast, looks preternaturally youthful, with big brown soulful eyes and full lips.

When I first saw the mugshots they had been online for just over an hour, and within minutes of clocking Su's face and *kunya* I had doubts about the YPG's claim that he was an American. Just days earlier the Syrian Democratic Forces (SDF), under whose auspices the YPG functions, had made the same claim about Zaid Abdul Hamid: the portly Trini who had appeared in an official ISIS video claiming that he couldn't practice his *"deen* 100%" back in Trinidad. The SDF captured Hamid fighting alongside the American Warren Christopher Clark,[4] who was later to relay in an interview on NBC news that he was curious to see "what the group [ISIS] was about," which was an odd thing to say given that ISIS, since at least 2014, was all over social media telling the world, in hate-filled rhetoric, exactly what it was about.[5]

It didn't take long to establish what I had suspected: that Su-lay—the correct spelling of his name—was also a Trini. He was taken to Syria on September 3, 2014, by his mother Gailon Su, in a party of nine, headed by his stepfather Anthony Hamlet, who had appeared in the same official ISIS video as Hamid.[6] Hamlet's last address in Trinidad was Hibiscus Arch Road, Rio Claro, which is on Imam Nazim Mohammed's settlement. Su-lay was just 12 years of age when he arrived in Syria.

I shared this information with Rukmini Callimachi, who works the terrorism beat at the *New York Times*. "Omg ['Oh my God']," she instantly fired back in an email, "if they [the SDF] misidentify another American I'm going to lose it."

A few days later Callimachi, with Eric Schmitt, published a story revealing Su-lay's nationality and identity. "The 16-year-old, who was erroneously identified in a news release from the American-backed militia as Soulay Noah Su, an American citizen, is actually Su-lay Su from Trinidad," Callimachi and Schmitt wrote, having received further confirmation from Su's sister Sarah Lee Su.[7]

It subsequently transpired that Su-lay had been captured alongside Gailon Su. According to the Dutch journalist Ana van Es, who had briefly spoken to Gailon after she had been put into custody and separated from Su-lay, they had surrendered to the SDF together. Gailon told van Es that Hamlet had "tricked" her into going to Syria.

She also said that within months of arriving in Syria she had divorced him, marrying another ISIS fighter soon after. And just like the first marriage, the second one didn't last either. "There is something wrong with them [ISIS fighters]. Troublesome men," she told van Es.[8] Gailon later relayed to *The New York Times* that she had married four men in Syria. "I was like a whore in the Dawla [the Islamic State]," she said.[9]

Judging by her Facebook page, Gailon was not your average "jihadi bride." For a start, she's a bit too old: 46. She had also come to Islam late in life, converting into the faith in 2014, when she was 42. And she was a former beauty queen (in one photo she posted in 2013 she is wearing a ribbon with "Miss Longdenville" printed on it). Nor was she your average ISIS homemaker: "She's intriguing," van Es told me, "I mean, her whole story is intriguing. It's not every day that you get a divorce inside the caliphate. I know that it was allowed, but it's unusual to do it twice."

To better understand Gailon I spoke with her 23-year-old daughter Sarah Lee Su, who lives in Trinidad and is not a Muslim. She was reluctant to speak about her relationship with Gailon, whom she last lived with when she was 16, but it was clear from what she said, or rather didn't say, that the relationship wasn't exactly a cloudless one. She said even less about her and Su-lay's biological father, a Chinese national, who she hasn't seen in fourteen years. "She didn't ask to go [to] Syria," Sarah said of her mother, clarifying that "the guy [Hamlet] she married told her that they were going to Mecca. I just want them to come back home, because, at the end of the day, my mum and my little brother is innocent."

I asked Sarah if her mother was a true believer in the ISIS ideology. Apparently she was not, and she had never been radicalized. Yet there she was in eastern Syria, hanging on to the bitter end among the last pockets of ISIS resistance. And Hamlet was no mere cook or farmhand conscripted into ISIS: he was a foreign fighter who had appeared in the group's official propaganda, and he was a core member of the ISIS hub in Rio Claro. I didn't want to press the issue with Sarah, but I found it difficult to imagine that Hamlet's beliefs and religious activism would have been hidden from Gailon, or that he would have married her had they not agreed on some fundamental jihadist precepts.

In an audio message Gailon had sent via Facebook Messenger a month before she was captured, she told Sarah, "Everyone wants to be blaming me, that I did bad things to my children. I just married a man." Which excuses all, but explains nothing.

The question of Su-lay's moral culpability is far easier to answer: he doesn't have any. He was 12 years of age when he was taken to Syria with his new family. So he didn't have any say in the matter. And as soon as he entered ISIS territory he would have been indoctrinated into the group's ideology and its theology of slaughter and self-sacrifice. He would have been subjected to grueling physical training in a military camp in preparation for fighting or "martyrdom operations" on the frontline. And, as an ultimate test of loyalty, he may have had to execute a captive of ISIS. "He is 16-years-old," van Es said, referring to Su-lay, "and most of the [captured ISIS] school-boys I spoke to [in eastern Syria] had to join ISIS at around 8, 9, 10, so it's likely that Su-lay was fighting for them [ISIS]."[10]

This, no doubt, makes Su-lay a potential "security risk" and explains why Western governments are so hesitant to take back their nationals who joined ISIS. But it also makes him a victim as much as a perpetrator in the Syrian jihad. ISIS not only brutalized Su-lay; they also stole his childhood, irrevocably.

On July 4, 2013, Gailon posted on Facebook a photo of Su-lay wearing a white untucked shirt with his arms crossed, leaning slightly back with his head to one side. He looks confident, a very cool customer indeed. The caption above the picture reads: "Yes!!! He did it again. Congrats to my son Su-lay for coming 1st in his end of term test and to all the proud mothers out there." It is hard and sobering to reconcile this photo of Su-lay with the mugshot of his older, but still all-too young, self taken by the YPG on the day of his capture.

\*\*\*

Muhammad Roach was even younger than Su-lay when his mother, a woman named Tricia Ramirez, took him to Syria in November 2014 with his then-14-year-old sister Qadirah.

In early 2016 I met Muhammad and Qadirah's father, Marvin Roach, who agreed to speak to me about the abduction of his two children. We met in a food court above Frederick Street in Port of Spain, near where Marvin works in a mobile phone store. It was June, and still Ramadan, and hot as hell.

As we sat down I asked Marvin—carelessly—if he wanted a drink. He politely declined: he was fasting. Marvin, like so many black African Muslims in Trinidad, is a convert. Born in 1974 in San Juan, just outside Port of Spain, he was 19 when he converted from Christianity to Islam. His teenage years, he told me, were "a little wild: *liming*, partying, having fun, Carnival." It wasn't a straight conversion because his first introduction to Islam was via the Nation of Islam, the controversial African-American religious group led by Louis Farrakhan. But after visiting a "real mosque" in Trinidad and "seeing what it's really like," he soon discovered that "they [the Nation of Islam] were preaching stuff that contradicts the true Islam." This "real mosque" was Nur-E-Islam, in El Socorro, San Juan, one of the largest in the country, and the same mosque attended by Shazam Mohammed, who was among the first cohort of Trinis to join ISIS in July 2014. (Shazam left Trinidad around the same time as his friend Zaid Abdul Hamid, with whom he appeared in the 2014 *Eid Greetings from the Land of Khilafah* video.)

The reason I offered Marvin a drink is because when he approached me his eyes were crimson and wet, and I didn't know what else to say. At the University of Kent, where I teach a Master's course on research methods and ethics, I urge my students to try to develop rapport with interviewees before asking questions: joke, mess around, loosen it up. But how are you supposed to do that with a man who has lost his two children—his only children—to a war zone and a group that rapes girls[11] and turns boys into human bombs,[12] all as a matter of deliberate policy?

To say that Marvin finds this a difficult subject is an understatement. So the first question I asked him was about his ex-wife, to whom he had been married for just over ten years and who he divorced in 2011. This was safer ground, because it wasn't Muhammad and Qadirah, and because it allowed Marvin to feel his way toward a different order of emotion. Tricia, his ex, he said, was "a very pig-headed, very arrogant person ... not someone who could be easily advised." Like Marvin, she too was a convert, becoming a Muslim when she was around 13, after moving in with her aunt, who was also a Muslim. But unlike Marvin, who is devout, Tricia, he said, "would dress the part and everything, but I wouldn't really call her religious." She was also, in Marvin's telling, an unreliable and chaotic mother, often turning up to the kids' school to collect them as classes were still in progress. The man she left Marvin for and remarried—Sean Bartholomew (AKA Shabazz Ali)—was also hardly a role model: he was an ex-con and he was violent. Marvin recalled that just after he had won custody of the children, Bartholomew came to his store and attacked him with a metal bar. Bartholomew was arrested and charged for this, but the case was dropped because of a procedural error.

As part of the divorce settlement, Marvin was given sole custody of the children, but Tricia was allowed to have them one weekend a fortnight. When Tricia collected the children on Friday, November 21, 2014, a date that is seared into Marvin's memory, she told him that she was taking them to Tobago for the weekend and would return them to school on Monday. But when Monday came, Muhammad and Qadirah were nowhere to be seen. Around lunchtime, Tricia sent Marvin a text, explaining that she was extending their stay in Tobago and would return on Thursday. Straight away, Marvin felt that "something's not adding up." And he was right: Thursday came, and Tricia and the children were still gone, and now she wasn't responding to his calls and texts. He then contacted child services and the police, who on searching Tricia's home found her two older sons, both in their early twenties, from a previous relationship, but not Tricia or Muhammad and Qadirah. It transpired that Tricia, on the day before she was due to return the children, had taken them on a flight bound for Suriname and, eventually, to Turkey. This was despite Marvin having the children's passports, which they would have needed to fly. Marvin believes that Tricia, in planning the abduction, had bribed an official to acquire new passports for the children. Not only did he have Muhammad and Qadirah's passports; he also had their birth certificates. "*Yuh* cannot get a passport without a valid birth certificate," he said.

According to Marvin, when the police arrived at Tricia's house, they seized the cell phone of one of the sons, but it had just been wiped and revealed nothing. They also questioned the sons about the whereabouts of their mother, but to no avail: "Police didn't get anything out of them." Around the same time, the police paid Marvin a visit: "A couple of investigators came by, they took statements and that was it. No follow-up. No nothing." And it has been like that ever since, Marvin said. "No updates. *Nutting*. I honestly don't know what they doing, what information they have, what they gathered, I don't know."

It was through his own investigations that Marvin was able to piece together what had happened. Tricia's new husband Sean Bartholomew, Marvin told me, had taken a flight from Trinidad on October 8, 2014, to Suriname, and from there onto Turkey, where he made his way to Syria to join ISIS. This was confirmed in a fifty-page leaked document from a T&T police agency, reported on in the *T&T Guardian* in April 2016.[13] Marvin was also able to locate Bartholomew's Facebook page, where he found photos of Bartholomew posing with Tricia in Syria. He also found out about Bartholomew's death, subsequently confirmed in the *T&T Guardian*, coming across his "martyrdom" picture on social media before this was public knowledge.

Bartholomew, as Marvin describes him, was a troubled soul. The two knew each other well and used to be friends. Born in Trinidad, he moved to the United States when he was four, returning in his early forties after being deported for drugs offenses there. "First impression was jail-bird, his whole demeanor," said Marvin, recalling the first time they met, having been introduced by a mutual friend who asked Marvin to take him to a mosque. "He told me, 'I really don't have no friends in

Trinidad, I've been away, I really lonely, could you befriend me?' Just like that." And just like that, Marvin befriended him. "I got his first job for him," Marvin said. "I remember even giving him clothes." Marvin also tried advising him on matters of faith: "I started teaching him stuff, because I realised his knowledge was very limited Islamically." But little of what Marvin told him seemed to get through. "He was very arrogant, hasty, short fuse," Marvin recalled, adding that "it wasn't far-fetched to see a person like him becoming involved in stuff like this," referring to his involvement with militant Islam and ISIS. It was through Marvin that Bartholomew met Marvin's then-wife Tricia.

Unlike some Muslims I'd spoken to in Trinidad about ISIS, Marvin was clear-eyed and firm on the matter: "Only stupid people get involved in ISIS. The majority of people being killed at the hand of ISIS are Muslim! You leavin' Trinidad, a beautiful country, sun 24-7, beaches nice, coconut water, *doubles*, we live good here, nobody stop us from practicing our religion. You free ... You would give up all of this to go in a so-called holy war, where the majority of the people you're killing are Muslim."

A lot of Trinis in Syria and Iraq, Marvin told me, are gang members with pending court cases back in Trinidad. Some of them he personally knew. "One guy that I know very well, he's a drug-addict. I know him from being strung out on crack-cocaine to being a soldier for ISIS." Many other brothers he knew would just disappear, turning up weeks later in news coverage of foreign fighters in Syria. "They in the gym, you're working out, there's brother so-and-so—'Hey, how are you?' Next thing you missed the brother for a couple of weeks and then later you're watching the same person on the news. These guys just buying tickets and walking out of Trinidad. No one stops them."

I asked Marvin if he had contemplated going to Turkey or Syria to try to find Muhammad and Qadirah. He has, but he told me that it wasn't a good idea, because of the dangers involved, and that in any case he didn't have the money for the trip. He also said that not a single day goes by when he doesn't think about Muhammad and Qadirah. Only in his dreams does he get to see them and hear their voices: "It's always, like, they return, always them coming back."

A few days after I'd interviewed Marvin, he sent me a photograph of Muhammad and Qadirah, sitting in the back of his car. Muhammad is in a blue shirt, with the beginnings of a smile on his face. Qadirah is wearing a white hijab, with a large daisy attached to it, and two more on her top. They both look happy and full of promise.

It is a very different photo from the ones I later came across on Qadirah's Facebook page, where she calls herself "Lioness of Sham [Syria]." The last time she updated her profile picture was on May 23, 2016. She is standing at the edge of a river in a black *burka*. Not even her eyes are visible. The photo attracted sixty "likes," including ones from her mother Tricia and Aliya Abdul Haqq.

Further down the page two other photos appear, both posted in 2015. One is of Qadirah holding an AK47. It is captioned: "Got plenty toys.... But this one is my favorite 💖😁☺️🔫." The weapon, against jihadi convention, is pointing away from her reproductive organs. The other photo is of Qadirah cradling the same weapon with her gloved-finger on the trigger. This, too, is captioned: "Dawlatul Islam Baqiyah🔫✏️💣 #AllahAkbar ["God is Great"]. "Dawlatul Islam" denotes Islamic State, while "baqiyah" is the first part of the ISIS slogan "Baqiyah wa Tatamadad," which means "remaining and expanding."

It is easy to be outraged by these photos and the captions attached to them. But Qadirah was just 15 years old in 2015, so the outrage should be aimed not at her but at the woman who indoctrinated her. On July 10, 2014, she posted a photo of a niqabed-up Tricia. Above it she wrote: "My Mother Is the Most Beautiful Woman I Ever Saw. All I Am I Owe to My Mother. I Attribute My Success in Life to the Moral. Intellectual [guidance?] I Received from Her." It is impossible not to be moved by the naivety of this—and at the magnitude of just how wrong Qadirah was.

As I write this, in January 2019, the whereabouts of Muhammad and Qadirah remains unknown, but, according to an anonymous source, Tricia is still alive, holed up somewhere in Syria with her new husband—Anthony Hamlet.

\*\*\*

Marvin Roach is not the only parent in Trinidad to have had his children abducted by an ex-partner and taken to Syria. A woman named Felicia Perkins-Ferreira, whom Marvin knew and told me about when I interviewed him, had also been subjected to this ordeal, although their stories are very different.

In June 2014 Felicia's ex-partner, Abebe Oboi Ferreira, took Mahmud (then 7) and Ayyub (then 3) to Syria, where they settled in Raqqa with their Belgian stepmother. They remained there until October 2017, when, just as Raqqa was about to fall,[14] their father told them to flee toward Turkey, while he would stay to fight to the end in defense of the caliphate's *de facto* capital. He was soon killed, but Mahmud and Ayyub survived—just about. Their stepmother abandoned them on the side of the road as she fled, where they were later picked up by SDF troops and taken to Camp Roj in northern Syria—a grim holding facility for ISIS-affiliated women and children. Journalists Bethan McKernan and Joshua Surtees broke the story about Mahmud and Ayyub in the British *Guardian* in December 2018.[15] According to Felicia, her ex-husband had taken the boys to Syria without telling her. "When they left, he [Abebe Oboi Ferreira] told me they were going to their grandmother's house. The next day my sister came and she said he'd gone to Syria … It wasn't until a bit later I felt this emptiness and broke down crying," she told McKernan and Surtees. Oddly, the story had nothing more to relay about Felicia, neglecting to elaborate on who she was and what (if anything) she had done over the last four years to try and bring her children back to Trinidad. But it did mention that Reprieve, an international legal action charity that has represented people on death row and Guantanamo Bay detainees, had taken on the case of repatriating the two children, and it did take a glancing swipe at the T&T government, which it claimed had "shown little interest in reuniting the family." It also quoted Prime Minister Rowley, who reportedly told Surtees, "We don't have the machinery or the wherewithal to identify people and bring them back."

Rowley's government may not have had the "wherewithal" to bring Mahmud and Ayyub back, but Reprieve clearly did. On

January 21, 2019, Felicia was reunited with her two sons in north-east Syria, after Reprieve had spent months negotiating their handover. She was accompanied by Reprieve's Clive Stafford Smith, as well as Surtees, who covered the story with McKernan for *The Guardian*.[16] The whole operation was bankrolled by Roger Waters, a former member of the now defunct rock band Pink Floyd, who also supplied a private jet to fly the party from Iraq to Switzerland. "We're going to make sure that they get on with a really productive, decent life," Stafford Smith told *The Guardian*, which relayed that "Ayyub dreams of being a professional footballer and Mahmud wants to become a cricketer."[17]

The story attracted international attention.[18] It also entrained a minor controversy in T&T about the government's role in repatriating the children. According to Stafford Smith, in a letter published in *T&T Newsday*, the T&T government was worse than useless in facilitating the return of Ayyub and Mahmud to Trinidad.[19] He did, however, express his thanks to T&T civil servants for their assistance in speedily arranging the necessary documents to enable the boys to travel. Stafford Smith's letter was a direct response to a press release on January 22, 2019, by the government, which stated that it had known about the case of the two children and had launched an investigation into it as far back as August 2018.[20] This investigation, according to the press release, was led by "a multidisciplinary and multiagency" unit called "the Nightingale Team," whose role is to "deal with possible repatriation and reintegration of citizens of Trinidad and Tobago who have been held in refugee and detention camps in Syria and Iraq." The team, the press release noted, was established in August 2018, but it wasn't until the January 22 press release that its existence was first made public. The press release also made it clear that the "Nightingale Team" had contacted Felicia about Ayyub and Mahmud, but that it was rebuffed: "It is noteworthy that her response was not an enthusiastic one and there was no record of her reporting that the children had been abducted by their father and taken to Syria (or even out of Trinidad and Tobago)."[21] This seems to be a direct and deliberate riposte to both McKernan and Surtees's claim in their first *Guardian* report that the T&T government had "shown little interest in reuniting the family";[22] and it flatly contradicted a claim Felicia had made in the *T&T Newsday* on January 4, 2019, where she said: "It seems like they [the T&T government] don't care. They never called or asked to see me. I've been waiting years to hear anything from them and it's always the same story and I'm tired. If it wasn't for the journalists and Clive taking on my story, I would have been still waiting for them to acknowledge me."[23] The same article records that "Perkins-Ferreira says she made a report about the abduction of her children in 2014, at the Four Roads Police Station [in Diego Martin]."

Stafford Smith didn't hold back in his letter to *T&T Newsday*. He described the government's press release as "insulting drivel."[24] He lambasted the suggestion that "Felicia did not show enough interest in getting their [the government's] help for her children," and then pointed out how "utterly useless these people have been in achieving anything for her over the four years of her torment." "But most important," he wrote, "I want to be absolutely clear: Felicia Perkins-Ferreira is herself a victim, desperate for four years to get her children back … For your officials to imply somehow that she did not care is simply disgusting."

A day after Stafford Smith's letter was published, Stuart Young, the new Minister of National Security (he replaced Edmund Dillon in August 2018), made a statement in which he reiterated that the authorities were not able to find any record of a police report being made in 2014 about the abduction of Felicia's two boys. He said by way of further clarification: "When we began the conversation at the outset of the investigations as to 'Would you be prepared to take the children back? Would you be able (allow) an assessment of the environment if the children are to return?', we found that she [Felicia] did not seem to be in any level of anxiety or had any level of wanting to get the children back in a hurry."[25] Young also reportedly "implied that it was only when there was a change of status in the mother's personal life and the media got on to the story that the modus operandi of the mother changed."[26]

This is certainly consistent with what Marvin Roach had told me about Felicia in June 2016: that she hadn't reported her children missing.

Felicia's case came up when I asked Marvin if he knew of any other parents in his situation. He told me that he'd tried to contact Felicia, but that she wasn't interested in speaking with him. He also spoke of the costs of speaking out, which stunned me because it seemed impossible that anyone could take issue with Marvin's right to publicize the horror of what he'd been through in an effort to pressure the authorities to try and retrieve his children. But many people did take issue with it, Marvin told me. He was attacked on social media, for "selling out" and "doing Muslims wrong by airing their dirty washing" in public; and some told him that Tricia was right in taking the children to the caliphate. Marvin, who is clearly tough and thick-skinned, shrugged all this off, but he spoke with great eloquence and power about just how corrosive and misguided was the code of *omertà* that operates in some Muslim communities in Trinidad: "People here need to let go of this allegiance," he said. "'I know he doing wrong, eh, but he's my friend so I wouldn't tell on him', 'I don't support what he doing, eh? But I will still hide his secrets'—Muslims need to stop this." Referring to Felicia, Marvin said, "She never went to the news media, probably because she saw what happened to me."

So it is possible that the reason Felicia went to neither the police nor the press about the abduction of her children is that she was afraid and didn't want to expose herself to potential ostracism from the Muslim community in which she lived. It is also possible that had she done so her ex-partner, Abebe Oboi Ferreira, whom she relied on to stay in contact with Ayyub and Mahmud, may have severed contact with her.

Was Felicia, as Stafford Smith insisted in his letter to *T&T Newsday*, a victim? Or was she, as Young insinuated, a negligent mother who should have reported the abduction of her two children to the police? The answer is probably a great deal more complex than both of these contrasting viewpoints would suggest. Looking through her numerous Facebook accounts—I identified seven—I was struck by just how intimately connected Felicia was with core members of the Trini ISIS mujahideen, including Aliya Abdul Haqq, Tricia Ramirez, and Nuru Muhammad, who was a promising professional footballer in T&T before he left for Syria in October 2014.[27] Nuru, however, was not always exactly friendly. On May 8, 2015, Felicia wrote the following post:

I was talking to myself yesterday saying i needs to get married so i asked allah plz send me a nice bro with understanding. So i left work with my girl going in a car forgot my bag, jump out running back with my big ass slowing me down almost reached my destination a brother asked me if i want a drop kindly accepted. Reached he asked if he could wait on me because of the outers men up there. Proceeding back to where i was going we chat. Reached salaam on my way to the maxi he called me back for my num. So u see allah is answering my call and im grateful to know im appreciated and allah loves me even on my offtimes ameen.

Nuru, who would have read this in his downtime from fighting on the frontlines with ISIS in Syria, was outraged by this show of permissiveness on Felicia's part—or so he saw it. "Whoever supports this," he thundered, "seek refuge in Allah, this status is shameful and nothing to do with Islam." By "this," he meant Felicia accepting a lift from a male who wasn't her husband or a relative.

Felicia clearly knew many hardcore jihadists, but there is little to suggest that she was a hardcore ISIS supporter herself. In fact, far from being a dogmatic purveyor of any ideology, the overwhelming impression she gives in her social media postings is of someone confused, chaotic, and lost. In one post, dated February 8, 2014, she shared a photo of a voluptuous naked female bottom. In another, dated September 18, 2014, she uploaded a photo of a niqabed-up female jihadi shooting an AK47. It is hard to think of two more starkly discrepant images of female empowerment.

In one particularly poignant Facebook post, dated August 2, 2015, Felicia berated herself for not doing more to protect her two children. It makes for difficult reading: "Everyday i pray allah by boys to be safe and secure cause its hard for me not being able to see them again ... Mahmud Ayyub mummy loves u guys so much and sorry she didnt see the signs to protect u gives im sorry and with allah could forgive me ... "

***

Ayyub and Mahmud are now in T&T with Felicia and her new husband. Despite the terrible things they must have seen and experienced in Syria, they are the lucky ones: they made it back. It is hard to quantify with any real certainty, but it's likely that more than 100 Trini minors were taken to Syria or Iraq between 2014 and 2016; and probably around thirty children were born to Trini parents in those two countries.

In February 2019 *Sky News* interviewed a female detainee at the Kurdish-run Al-Hol camp in north-eastern Syria. Speaking with a Caribbean accent and in a voice seething with anger and not a little entitlement, she said, "I would like to hear Trinidad's view on the people who are here. There are over 90 Trinidadian children in Syria. Ninety kids. Do they care? Are they even concerned?"[28]

According to "Concerned Muslims of T&T," an activist group that is calling for the repatriation of all Trini women and children detained in Syria and Iraq, there are forty children and sixteen women in the Al-Hol camp alone.[29] A recent news story in *Middle East Eye*, dated November 15, 2019, claimed that the number of Trini nationals in this camp is more than double this.[30] According to journalist Amandla Thomas-Johnson, "some 25 women and 71 child nationals of Trinidad and Tobago were at the [Al-Hol camp] as of the start of November." Nineteen of the Trini children were reportedly born in Syria. Thomas-Johnson also noted that "22 other children are held in Iraq." Based on discussions I've had with security sources in Trinidad and journalists on the ground in Syria I would say that these figures are more or less accurate.

(Of the 72,000 residents in the Al-Hol camp, about two-thirds are children.[31])

In answer to the female detainee's rhetorical question, "Are they even concerned?": Well, yes, Trinis *are* concerned, and many *do* in fact care about the Trini kids and their parents out in Syria and Iraq. They care very deeply, but not in the way that this woman demands or expects. Which is to say that they strongly believe that anyone from Trinidad who left to join ISIS should never be allowed to return to the country ever again. As one Trini pungently put it in a Facebook comment below a news story about a Trini woman's plea to come home from Syria,[32] "Soooooo ..... you went to do your SHIT overseas get your ass in jail and now you want the state with our facking money to bail your ass out and bring you back steuppps." And this, broadly or in spirit at least, is the current position of the T&T government: *you can come back, but we're not going to help you to do so.* Just as it buried its head in the sand when its citizens were going to Syria and Iraq between 2014 and 2016, the government is more or less doing the same about those now hoping to make the reverse journey. T&T of course is not alone here: many other Western governments have done the same and a few, most notably Britain and the United States, have outright refused to take back some ISIS-affiliated nationals, stripping them of their citizenship.[33]

The number of male Trinis currently in detention in Syria and Iraq remains unclear, although four men can definitely be accounted for: Zaid Abdul Hamid, Safraz Ali, Nicholas Joseph Lee (AKA Abu Yousuf al-Amriki),[34] and Ziyad Mohammed. The total number of Trini male detainees is likely to be higher, but one should bear in mind that many were killed in combat in Syria and Iraq. (According to an anonymous source from within the T&T Ministry of National Security, as of January 2018, a total of thirty Trini adult males had been killed in Syria and Iraq.)

As far as I know, only one adult male has returned to Trinidad. He left in November 2014, but returned at some point in 2015. He is currently in prison on charges relating to a robbery. This is not public knowledge in the country.

Among the female contingent, one woman and her two teenage stepdaughters have returned to Trinidad.[35] According to T&T's Counter Trafficking Unit, this woman was duped by her husband—Anthony Hamlet—into going to Syria: she thought she was going on a family vacation.[36] (Hamlet had two wives, but, unlike his second wife, Gailon Su, this one left Syria with her two girls soon after arriving there.)

In Western Europe, by contrast, nearly 800 males have returned.[37] Hence Trinidad, at present, doesn't have a returnee problem. But this is likely to change, given that the SDF cannot reasonably be expected to house thousands of ISIS-affiliated foreign women and children indefinitely and because the political and security situation in eastern Syria remains so volatile.

In December 2015 it was reported that four Trini males were among 961 persons held at the Turkish border by Turkish authorities.[38] And in January 2018 Edmund Dillon disclosed to the T&T parliament that, following ISIS's territorial defeats in Mosul and Raqqa, a group of Trinis were being held at a detention camp in Iraq.[39] Aneesa Waheed, the daughter of Nazim Mohammed, and her husband Daud Waheed were among this group. In April 2018 Aneesa Waheed was sentenced to twenty years imprisonment by a court in Baghdad.[40] Nazim Mohammed, Aneesa's father, believes that Daud has been executed.

In addition to the hundreds of Trinis who traveled to Syria and Iraq, there are many who tried to go, but failed and remain in T&T. Among them are twelve Trini nationals who were captured trying to cross the border into Syria by the Turkish authorities in July 2016. They were deported back to T&T in April 2017.[41] There are probably many more who wanted to leave, but for whatever reason couldn't or chose not to do so.

In the aftermath of ISIS's territorial defeat in Syria and Iraq, the question of whether its foreign supporters will turn their attention to carrying out attacks in their home countries warrants serious consideration. Since late 2014, when scores of countries joined together in a global coalition against ISIS, the group has been actively plotting and inciting attacks against the members of this coalition. Indeed this was one of Crawford's central messages to "the Muslims of Trinidad" in his interview with *Dabiq* in 2016. "I also say to you, my brothers, that you now have a golden opportunity to do something that many of us here wish we could do right now," he said. "You have the ability to terrify the disbelievers in their own homes and make their streets run with their blood ... Attack the interests of the Crusader coalition near you, including their embassies, businesses, and 'civilians' ..."[42]

According to the researcher Robin Simcox, in the twenty-nine months between January 2014 and May 2017, there were 142 Islamist plots, targeting fifteen different European countries, resulting in 327 deaths.[43] In Trinidad over the same period there have been no attacks and just one plot in February 2018, although, as we have seen, the circumstances surrounding the latter still remain controversial.

It is hard to know if this picture will change. One cop I spoke to was emphatic on the matter: "It's just a matter time," he said, responding to my question about the threat of ISIS-inspired terrorism in T&T. He did add, however, that "since 1990 law enforcement is better prepared." When I posed the same question to Daurius Figueira, the T&T criminologist, he wasn't so sure. He pointed out that the blowback from any terrorist attack on a domestic target in T&T would be so overwhelming and costly that no sane person or group would even think about doing it. Figueira's point left me feeling uneasy, particularly about the wave of repression and enmity that would crash down on Muslim communities in T&T were some of its fringe members stupid enough to try and launch a terrorist attack on the island. You sense that things could escalate very fast and very bad, resulting in a convulsion of the magnitude of the 1990 attempted coup. This is every Trinis worst nightmare—bar getting killed, robbed, kidnapped, or raped. And it's why the memory of the coup still lives on in T&T, because the fear is that history will repeat itself in some form or other.

*\*\*\**

Like most Western states, the T&T government has shown little political will in seeking to address the returnee issue, and has been largely non-committal in its approach.[44] But there is increasing pressure on it to change course and bring home all the ISIS-affiliated Trini women and children. At the time of writing, the Islamic Front leader Umar Abdullah is advocating for legal action to compel the government to repatriate all Trini women and minors in detention in Syria.[45] Internationally, too, pressure is mounting, with Turkey promising to deport foreign ISIS-detainees in its custody, following its recent incursion into Kurdish territory.[46]

There are no easy solutions to the whole returnee problem, and it raises a number of complex questions to do with justice, cost, and security.

On the matter of justice, the case for the repatriation of Trini minors is a strong one, since they didn't choose to go to Syria to join ISIS. This makes them victims and the T&T government has a duty to bring them home. But one shouldn't be under any illusions about the challenges involved in returning them to Trinidad and providing them with the support that they will need. They will have been brutalized by their exposure to war, and many will have been indoctrinated into ISIS's brutal sectarian ideology. A huge investment of expertise and money will be required to care for and rehabilitate these children and teenagers. And some, particularly the male teenagers, may pose a security threat, given their combat experience.

The case for repatriating Trini women is also a strong one, given that it is indefensible to expect the Kurds to house them indefinitely and that the demands of justice require that they should be brought back to Trinidad, where they must face censure for their role in supporting a genocidal terrorist group and for exposing their children to the perils of a warzone.

Imam Sheraz Ali has suggested that many ISIS-affiliated Trini women were coerced or threatened into joining ISIS by their husbands. Ali has also remarked that there is no evidence that any Trini women took part in the fighting in Syria and Iraq.[47]

While it is possible that some Trini women may have been coerced into going to Syria or Iraq, many were die-hard supporters of ISIS who *wanted* to join the group; and, far from being "groomed" or "misled" into joining, they were, in fact, actively cheerleading for ISIS on social media before they left Trinidad. The idea they didn't know what they were getting themselves into is contemptible. Furthermore, the fact, if it is a fact, that the Trini women didn't fight on the battlefield, or keep Yazidi slaves, shouldn't detract from the central role that these women played is ISIS, given that, as wives and mothers, they not only actively supported their combatant-husbands but also acted as the incubators for the new generation of ISIS militants.

If the Trini women are to be repatriated, the authorities will not be able to charge them under current T&T Anti-Terrorism legislation, since the new laws, which proscribe ISIS as a terrorist group and hinder travel to jihadi hotspots abroad,[48] cannot be applied retroactively. But these women shouldn't be allowed to return to T&T without consequence, much less be treated as if they are benign victims. Three things, in fact, should happen if they do return: first, the authorities must assess the potential security threat that these women pose; second, the authorities must separate the women from their children, until it can be determined that they are fit parents; and third, the authorities should investigate the women for breaching international human trafficking law, to which T&T is a signatory.[49] It is well-documented that ISIS was conscripting boys into combat[50] as young as 10[51] and girls into marriages (and sexual servitude) as young as 9.[52] The degree to which the Trini women knew this, or were reckless as to what was going on in Syria or Iraq, is a question for the courts to answer.

Thus far there have been no public calls in Trinidad for the repatriation of male ISIS-affiliated Trinis. But the government should be prepared for their possible return and put mechanisms in place for this. Clearly, these individuals will pose a grave security risk, given their extensive combat experience. They may also, just like their female counterparts, try to sow further discord once they return. Should they return to T&T, they must be rigorously assessed and closely monitored by the security services, and, where possible, tried for involvement in war crimes and for trafficking their children into ISIS.

Some male Trinis in detention in Syria have sought to deny or minimize their involvement in ISIS. For example, 39-year-old Safraz Ali claims that he didn't know about ISIS's beheading of Western hostages before he left Trinidad and that he hadn't fought on the battlefield for ISIS.[53] Many other Western ISIS-affiliated detainees have made similar pleas, insisting that they were misled into going to Syria and Iraq and that they were only cooks or farm-hands for ISIS. These claims must be treated with a great deal of skepticism, and are clearly intended to garner sympathy.

The T&T government must invest more resources into counter-terrorism. At present, counter-terrorism efforts are spearheaded by the SAA (Strategic Services Agency) and Special Branch, two branches of the state that do not always cooperate effectively and openly with each other. The Police Commissioner Gary Griffith has long called for a specialist unit devoted to monitoring and foiling terrorist threats. The case for introducing such a unit is now overwhelming.

In August 2018 the government passed legislation to clamp down on terrorist funding and to stop people from going to terrorist hotspots like Iraq and Syria. This, though late in coming, is to be commended. However, it has yet to fully address the issue of radicalization in the country. In America and Europe, governments have supported efforts to "counter-message" violent extremists and empower communities to protect themselves against the recruiters and radicals. Should the T&T government do the same? Perhaps, but it should tread carefully here, given that there is no evidence to show that "counter-messaging" actually works. It should also proceed with caution in who it enlists as community partners. Whatever it chooses to do on this front, its efforts should be carefully calibrated and focused exclusively on engaging those communities in which ISIS recruitment has been taking place and on the mosques—in Rio Claro, Chaguanas, and Diego Martin—most closely associated with the block migrations to Syria and Iraq. For too long the government has slept on the problem of violent extremism. It is time for it to take a more proactive and positive approach.

# Conclusion

> They does talk some nonsense
> Me ain't know wey they doing it for
> 'Bout so much violence
> Man, you would swear that we fighting war
> Of course, we have we delinquents to face
> But just like any other place
> Look, the things they does say bout here
> Is really too much for me to bear
> 
> Mighty Sniper, "Portrait of Trinidad," 1965

What is it about Trinidad that has made it such a powerhouse of ISIS recruitment? This is not an easy question to answer, and many of the standard explanations for radicalization and terrorism simply don't apply in the Trinidad case. The answer, for example, doesn't lie in poverty or deprivation,[1] because Trinidad is not by any stretch a poor or deprived country and because many of those Trinis who mobilized to join ISIS were well-off and came from well-respected families. Nor does the answer lie in displacement or rootlessness,[2] since all of the Trinis who joined ISIS were born in Trinidad and were not living in expatriate enclaves in an alien society that showed them little tolerance or understanding. Still less does the answer lie, *pace* the French sociologist Olivier Roy,[3] in the emergence of a youth subculture fixated on revolt and death: most of the Trinis who took their families to Syria or Iraq were well into their thirties. And many who made that momentous decision did so not to die but to live under the dominion of a sharia-based social system that they were convinced would meet all their material and spiritual needs.

Moreover, T&T is a democratic republic with regular elections, a plurality of political parties, a free press, and an independent judiciary: so whatever is causing radicalization in the country it isn't a deficit in democratic institutions.[4]

What about marginalization, yet another one of the go-to concepts in radicalization discourse?

According to economists Efraim Benmelech and Esteban F. Klor, "poor economic conditions do not drive participation [of foreign fighters] in ISIS."[5] On the contrary: many ISIS foreign fighters, they find, came from countries with high levels of economic development, low income inequality, and highly developed political institutions. So what did drive the flow of foreign fighters to ISIS? Benmelech and Klor's answer, in short, is "ideology and the difficulty [faced by Muslims] of assimilation into homogenous Western countries."[6] Elaborating on this, Benmelech and Klor conjecture that discrimination against first- or second-generation Muslim immigrants in Western countries "may strengthen [their] religious identity ... and eventually induce some of them to radicalization, resulting in an increase in the supply of foreign volunteers into ISIS."[7]

This is broadly in line with William McCants and Christopher Meserole's research on the disproportionately high numbers of jihadist foreign fighters from France and Belgium. The "best predictor" of foreign fighter radicalization, they argue, isn't a country's wealth, or how well-educated its citizens were, or how much Internet access they enjoyed, but rather whether their country of origin is Francophone. "As strange as it may seem," McCants and Meserole write, "four of the five countries with the highest rates of radicalization in the world are Francophone, including the top two in Europe (France and Belgium)."[8] Why is this? For McCants and Meserole, the answer lies in the stridency of French secularism, which alienates Muslims and makes them more susceptible to ISIS recruitment narratives. This stridency, they observe, was particularly evident in the campaigns against the veil across the Francophone world in 2010 and 2011.

While the marginal status of Muslims in secular Western European countries may arguably explain ISIS foreign fighter flows from those countries, it offers little help in understanding the high rate of ISIS foreign traveler mobilization in T&T, a country with a high GDP (indeed, by GDP per capita T&T is the third-richest country in the Americas) and an ethnically diverse population into which Muslims are reasonably well-integrated. There are no Muslim diaspora communities in T&T, no Muslim ghettoes seething with resentment against a "host" population of "militant secularists," no anti-Muslim politics of the far right and no muscular liberal calls for Muslim women to remove modesty clothing. (In Trinidad Muslim women and girls have been bathing fully covered at Maracas beach for years and nobody even notices, much less cares.) On the contrary, Trini Muslims, in the main, are well-assimilated into a society that remains culturally conservative and largely god-fearing. (Only 9 percent of the adult population identify as non-religious, compared to 34 percent in the United States.[9]) But just how well-assimilated were the disproportionate numbers of Afro-Trini Muslim converts who joined ISIS? Islam in Trinidad is divided among a wide spectrum of groups and sects, ranging from the Indian-dominated Sunni Anjuman Sunnat-ul-Jamaat Association, the largest and most influential Muslim organization in T&T,[10] to the Afro-dominated Jamaat al Muslimeen (JAM), a group that exists very much on the fringe and in tension with both the governing elites in Trinidad and the Islamic mainstream in the country. According to ex-JAM member Hasan Anyabwile, many black Trini Muslims feel excluded from the main Islamic organizations in T&T, due to racism, and do not feel respected as "true" Muslims. This explains, he suggested, why some of these black Muslims embrace radical forms of the faith, since doing so allows them to simultaneously reject mainstream (Indo-) Trini Islam and proclaim a greater Islamic authenticity over those who rejected them. But this explanation—a novel reformulation of Benmelech and Klor's thesis that foregrounds integration deficits *within* Muslim communities—only takes us so far. While it helps explain the appeal of radicalism for these doubly marginalized Black Trini Muslims, it explains neither why most of those from this particular demographic didn't mobilize to join ISIS nor why so many Indo-Trinis did so mobilize.

The central question that must be addressed is not why alienated young men in their early twenties with nothing to lose would be willing to join ISIS,[11] but why men and women in their mid-thirties, many with decent jobs and young families, would be willing to join the group. Much of the current discourse on radicalization, because of its overwhelming focus on violent extremism in Western Europe and North America, where the majority of violent extremists are much younger and from poor Muslim diaspora communities, isn't well-equipped to answer this question.

In May 2015 a family of twelve from Luton, England— including, according to the BBC, "a baby and two grandparents"[12]—made the journey to Syria.[13] In a letter explaining their decision to go, they said: "None of us were forced against our will." Indeed, in joining the caliphate they were now "free from the corruption and oppression of man-made law … in which a Muslim doesn't feel oppression when practicing their religion. In which a parent doesn't feel the worry of losing their child to the immorality of society. In which the sick and elderly do not wait in agony, tolerating the partiality of race or social class."[14]

Many Trinis who went to Syria and Iraq expressed the same thoughts and sentiments in their social media postings: that they wanted to live in an Islamic state where Islamic justice reigns and God's rule truly rules. At the same time they also expressed a profound spiritual disillusionment with their own society, which they saw as sexually permissive, corrupt, and lacking in any real value. The standard discourse on radicalization would classify this negative subjective state or feeling as a "push." But this, surely, is far too deterministic a metaphor for capturing this species of spiritual repulsion: for nothing about Trinidad made it morally repulsive to the Trinis who left the country to join ISIS; rather, these defectors actively sought to make it repulsive, due to their psychological investment in a puritanical and unforgiving ideology that gave them no choice but to find it repulsive. If they were repelled by Trinidad, it was because they *wanted* to be repelled. Indeed, far from being "pushed," it is more accurate to say that they *jumped*. As one Trini ISIS fighter put it in a Facebook post, imploring his fellow Trinis at home to join him in Syria, "I had a nice house, car nice job work in oil love fishing an sports like any other young person Allah he test u wit this dunya [life] so wats the matter wit u wats ur excuse for not leaving darul kuff ["land of disbelief"] an adhering to the Call of jihad fighting for Allah an[d] victory of Islam."

When I spoke with Marvin Roach about the motivations of Trini jihadists, he cited theological ignorance and stupidity, as if cogent religious knowledge was a firewall against violent extremism. But above all, he expressed bafflement as to how any sane person could leave the good life in Trinidad for war abroad. Marvin was right, or rather half-right: life for many Trinis is, in the main, good. But what he couldn't seem to grasp was that the good life in Trinidad was very precisely the life the Trini ISIS mujahideen couldn't abide. They may certainly have enjoyed aspects of that life, but it wasn't enough for them, and it certainly was no competition for the intoxicating pull of jihad: of life-and-death struggle, followed by eternal bliss.[15] To semi-plagiarize from George Orwell's 1940 review of Hitler's autobiography *Mein Kampf*,[16] whereas "sweet" Trinidad offers its citizens gorgeous sunsets, a good bit of *bacchanal* [drama and intrigue], and a decent *lime*, ISIS offered struggle, danger, and salvation. And the Trini ISIS mujahideen chose the latter.

But they did so not in circumstances of their own choosing. Those circumstances had to do with Trinidad's own unique recent political history, where a militant Salafi group was allowed to develop in the southeast of the country from the mid-1990s onward. Led by Imam Nazim Mohammed, this group was an offshoot of the JAM, which had attempted to overthrow the country in 1990. It was also far more radical than Yasin Abu Bakr's original group, both in its rejection of the idea of democratic politics and in its embracement of jihad and spiritual renewal as a way of life. Whereas Bakr spent much of his time, from at least 1995 onward, trying to win political power and accrue real estate, Nazim was engaged in proselytizing activities, making notable in-roads in Chaguanas and Diego Martin.

Just one week after the 2001 September 11 attacks, Nazim, then 60, told the *T&T Express* that "any Muslim who supports any kafir (non-Muslim) to fight against Afghanistan, that fight will be against Allah and his Messenger, Prophet Muhammed."[17] He was referring to the coming US invasion of Afghanistan, which was launched in October of that year to remove the Taliban from power. While he acknowledged that it was "unfortunate that something like that happened," referring to the killing of thousands of civilians on 9/11, he added: "But when something happens to you, whenever you are confronted with something you first have to check yourself to see what you are doing wrong." When asked if the attacks were justified, he said: "I would not know. In Islam it says that you don't kill old people, women and children in your battle." The report noted that Mohammed's mosque in Boos Village, according to Mohammed, had over 100 members. It also relayed his denial that he had any links with the Taliban, despite then being an avowed supporter of the group.

Nazim's contempt for America and its foreign policy, which he described in the *T&T Express* report as "anti-Islamic," has scarcely wavered over the ensuing years. Nor has his support for the idea of an Islamic state. While the degree of his influence should not be exaggerated, were it not for his radical activism over many years—as well as the state's toleration of this—it is likely that far fewer Trinis would have made it to Syria and Iraq on the frontlines in the civil war that raged there from 2013 on and is not yet over.

In "An Open Letter to Imam Nazim Mohammed & Shaykh Abdullah Faisal; You will be raised in chains," posted on Facebook on May 7, 2018, the former JAM member and Islamic scholar Hasan Anyabwile wrote:

> You [Nazim] and Shaykh Faisal of Jamaica are the main culprits, this is why the Prophet Muhammad (s) said that on the Day of Judgement the Imams, Amirs and Leaders will be raised in chains.

You will have to answer for all your irresponsible sermons, fatwa and opinions, you and Shaykh Faisal, who called for the death of anyone (meaning me) who didn't support ISIS and their bogus Khalif and Khalifate and that it was "halal" [permissible] to take their wives, who should divorce them and take their properties, that was the Fatwa in those heady days.[18]

I have heard many of Abdullah el-Faisal's sermons in support of jihad and ISIS, because they are (or were) all over the Internet, and I have seen his ruling, posted on Twitter on November 1, 2014, where he pronounces, "Any Muslim who doesnt give his Bayah [allegiance] to the Islamic State is a Munafiq [hypocrite] and his wife is haram [forbidden] for him." I have not heard Nazim speak from the pulpit in defense of ISIS, and if there are recordings of him doing so you will not find them on the Internet, because Mohammed doesn't use it for the purpose of proselytizing.

Nazim and el-Faisal may well be, as Anyabwile charges, "the main culprits" in helping foment radicalization in Trinidad, but they are not the only ones. Ashmead Choate was also a prolific radical who supported jihadist causes and who, unlike Nazim and el-Faisal, actually acted on his radical rhetoric and traveled to Iraq to join ISIS in July 2015. Choate was particularly influential in the Islamist milieu in Chaguanas and Diego Martin. For a period he was an ideological mentor to Crawford and his associates. A relative of Choate told me: "Some days it seemed that his entire day was on a phone. What I can say was that he knew practically all of the men who left for Syria." Choate was also very well-connected in the Middle East, having studied Islamic jurisprudence at the University of Medina in Saudi Arabia, and may have acted as a conduit between Trinis at home and ISIS members in Syria and Iraq. He would certainly have had the legitimacy, in the eyes of ISIS, to vouch for Trinis who aspired to join ISIS's ranks in Syria and Iraq.

According to Daurius Figueira, the broader backdrop of ISIS radicalization in T&T is the growth, since the 1990s, of Salafi fundamentalism in the country, which he directly attributes to Saudi proselytizing. "They've spent money and brought in all these Wahhabi scholars from Mecca," he said. "They've passed on the doctrine, then they've started to take the young males and send them to Mecca, and then they come back to Mecca and they continue, so now you don't even need to send missionaries again." The most visible sign of this infiltration, he said, is the hijab: before the Saudis' missionaries came, Muslim women in Trinidad didn't wear it, but now he said it's fairly commonplace. The former T&T politician Nafeesa Mohammed, in a recent talk at the University of the West Indies in Trinidad, echoed a similar concern about the impact of Saudi-funded Wahhabism on T&T Muslim communities: "There is a discernible turning point in our country from the days when we were basically a traditional moderate Muslim society with three or four main Muslim organisations to a point where now, there has been a rise of fundamentalism," she observed. "I have tried to link it to my own personal experiences at our Masjid and I can trace it to the day when Saudi Arabia became so very wealthy in the 1990s with the oil money that they started to pump money into the Western world, and a lot of the foreign ideologies then started to seep into our Masjid."[19]

For Trinis who want to distance themselves and their country from the stain of ISIS it is obviously tempting to see it as some sort of foreign importation, a pathogen from the outside. But this misses the crucial point that the roots of ISIS in Trinidad are intimately located in the recent history and domestic politics of that country. Radical ideologies, however alien or foreign to Trinidad, were interpreted by local militant Muslims for their own political purposes and these Muslims formed paramilitary style groups that were largely tolerated by the state as long as they didn't threaten its existence. So while the Trinidad case testifies to the genuinely global reach of ISIS, it also demonstrates that were it not for local actors and networks it is unlikely that ISIS's ideology would have taken root on the island.[20]

A growing body of research in terrorism studies suggests that social networks play a central role in facilitating radicalization and the mobilization of foreign fighters.[21] This book resoundingly supports this research. Everyone in Trinidad who left for Syria and Iraq was part of the same network of around 350–400 like-minded individuals from three main areas in Trinidad: Chaguanas, Diego Martin, and, most prominently, Rio Claro. Many of these individuals knew or were related to each other. No one self-radicalized, and no one left for Syria or Iraq without the ideological, emotional, and material support of the network. Moreover, the origins of this network long predated ISIS and can be traced to the fracturing, in the mid-1990s, of another militant Islamist group—the JAM. At the head of the network was a jihadi veteran—not of some distant jihad in foreign lands, but of the lesser-known jihad in Trinidad of July 1990. This veteran—Nazim Mohammed—was able to operate in Trinidad with almost total impunity, not only proselytizing across the country but also implementing an informal system of sharia law on his settlement in Rio Claro.

"Trinidad is my land, and of it I am proud and glad. But I can't understand why some people does talk it bad," croons Mighty Sniper in the 1965 calypsonian classic "Portrait of Trinidad."[22] "They would paint here black here every day. And the right things they would never say." The right thing to say of course is that Trinidad is a paradise that couldn't possibly produce something as monstrous as ISIS militants. But that would be a lie.

While Trinidad, or rather Tobago, where all the decent beaches in the country are, is a place of escape for holiday-makers from Europe and the United States, for the Trini ISIS mujahideen it became a place to escape *from*: a false paradise that could not compete with what the caliphate had to offer. How spectacularly wrong they were: not for seeing through the myth-making about their own country, but for credulously buying into the even greater myth-making of ISIS.

# Author's Note

When I first mentioned to my friend and journalist Andy Anthony that I was off to Trinidad to research ISIS radicalization there, he wished me luck and envied how, as he put it, I'd soon be kicking back "on the beach, under the tropical sun, drinking primary colored cocktails." Needless to say, Andy hasn't been to Trinidad.

This isn't to say that I didn't have some decent *limes* and fun while I was there; of course I did. But it wasn't all plain sailing, to use a clichéd if appropriate nautical metaphor.

Qualitative social scientists often make a big song and dance—think of former British Prime Minister Teresa May trying to bust some moves on a trip to Nairobi—about their research methods and "epistemic" orientations, droning on about how they enlisted a "gatekeeper" and what challenges they faced in what they reverentially call the "the field" (otherwise known as the world outside of the academic ivory tower). I have no time for all that, and suspect that you don't either. So let's not mystify the process: As a researcher you make some calls, try your luck and see what transpires, which is exactly what I did. You put yourself about—a lot—and you persist. Then you go home and write the thing up. This all takes a bit of time, and you keep doing interviews and speaking to people and reading until you think that you have enough.

Alas, I never did get to kick back and drink garish cocktails on an idyllic beach in T&T. Instead, I spent most of my time sweating my ass off in transit to an interview location, or freezing my ass off while conducting an interview (Trinis *love* air-conditioning), or hanging around for interviewees (who were no doubt sweating *their* asses off in traffic on route to meet me), or trying not to get robbed on the way back to my temporary crib after doing an interview.

In total, I conducted more than fifty semi-structured interviews in Trinidad over the course of eight two-week-long field trips between February 2016 and August 2018. I interviewed key figures in the

Islamic/Islamist milieu in T&T, including Imam Nazim Mohammed (head of the Umar Ibn Khattab mosque), Umar Abdullah (head of the Waajihatul Islaamiyyah (Islamic Front)), Kwesi Atiba (a former JAM member and imam at the Islamic Resource Center), Imtiaz Mohammed (president of the Islamic Missionaries Guild), Hasan Anyabwile (a UK-based sheikh and former member of the JAM), Fuad Abu Bakr (the son of the JAM's leader Yasin Abu Bakr), and Inshan Ishmael (head of the Muslim Social and Cultural Foundation). I visited several mosques in Trinidad, where I interviewed worshippers and imams and participated in Eid celebrations. I also interviewed an undercover police officer; a homicide police detective; the head of the T&T Police Service's Special Branch division, as well as several former members of that division; a lawyer who had represented a prominent Trini foreign fighter, three local journalists who have reported on Trini ISIS foreign fighters; a former Minister of National Security (Gary Griffith); a local criminologist who is an expert on jihadist discourse (Daurius Figueira); and several family members and friends of Trinis who joined and fought for ISIS.

Most of the interviews were recorded and transcribed, and some interviewees were interviewed more than once. Unfortunately I was not able to interview any Trini foreign fighters (when I first started conducting interviews in early 2016 most had been killed).

In addition to infield interviews in Trinidad, I spent hundreds of hours talking with sources—from both Muslim communities and the state security services—via an encrypted messaging service. I also interviewed several foreign-based journalists who had met and interviewed Trini ISIS members in camps in north-eastern Syria.

I leaned heavily on two sources of data on the demographic profiles of Trini ISIS travelers: a *T&T Guardian* news story on a leaked police file containing information on 102 of them; and a comprehensive database on 70 ISIS-affiliated individuals who left Trinidad between November 2013 and March 2015.

In compiling this database I was greatly helped by several anonymous T&T security sources, two local journalists, and several members of

T&T's Muslim communities. I also conducted a year-long investigation into the social media activities of ISIS supporters in T&T.

The book I have written is a short one, but in researching and writing it I have run up a long list of debts. First and foremost I would like to warmly thank everyone who gave up their time to speak to me about violent extremism in T&T. I cannot name all these generous souls, but I would like to extend a hearty big-up to each and every one of them.

I should particularly like to express my thanks to my colleagues at *The Atlantic*—Uri Friedman, Kathy Gilsinan, Juliet Lapidos, and Yoni Appelbaum—and to Cameron Abadi and David Kenner at *Foreign Policy*. Thanks, also, to Jamie Clifton at *Vice*, Susan Brenneman at the *Los Angeles Times*, Alicia Wittmeyer and Max Strasser at *The New York Times*, and Tom Goodenough at *The Spectator*.

For much help and support, I owe a special debt to my friends and colleagues from the UK Foreign and Commonwealth Office: Louise Barton, Martha Turnbull, Caroline Alcock, Maia Hibben, Fayola Fraser, and Tim Stew.

To the family and friends of Raoul Pantin (RIP): what a tremendous journalist and writer he was and how I would have loved to have met him.

For much buss-up-shut and curry shrimp, I humbly thank Wings Roti Shop in Tunapuna.

I would also like to thank: Aaron Zelin, Alex Meleagrou-Hitchens, Amandla Thomas-Johnson, Amarnath Amarasingam, Amnon Lev, Ana Van Es, Andre, Andrew Anthony, Aris Roussinos, Balihar Sanghera, Benedetta Argentieri, Benjie Mahabir, Brinsley Samaroo, Christopher Dickey, Chris Shilling, Daniel Byman (whose excellent book on foreign fighters—*Road Warriors*—came out just as I was finishing this one), Daurius Figueira, David Brotherton, David Toube, Dennis, Derek Chadee, Dipesh Gadher, Elke Van Hellemont, Finbar, Frank Furedi, Gail Alexander, Gary Griffith, Hasan Anyabwile, Jack Cunliffe, Joshua Surtees, Josie Ensor, Keith Hayward, Ken Roodal, Keron, Kevin M., Kevin Peters, Letta Tayler, Liam Duffy, Mark Bassant, Mark Hamm, Mia Boom, Mustafa Akyol, Nasser Mustafa, Nayiri Kendir, Phil Carney,

Roger S., Rukmini Callimachi, Sabrina Shroff, Seamus Hughes, Shashi Jayakumar, Stacy B., Steven Byers, Thomas Cushman, Thomas Hegghammer, Tomasz Hoskins, Umar Abdullah, Wladimir van Wilgenburg, Winston Carmichael, and Yuanbo Qi.

Thanks are also due to Bruce Hoffman for his sage advice and solid support, as well as to Phil Gurski for being in my corner and for his hard-earned wisdom on all terror-related matters.

Finally, I owe a special thanks to my *hoss* Azard Ali, whose warmth, encouragement, and Trini-to-the-bone aversion to bullshit helped me enormously throughout researching and writing this book, which is dedicated to him.

# Notes

## Prologue

1. Reshma Ragoonath and Shastri Boodan, "Highway Hit," *T&T Guardian*, November 25, 2013: http://www4.guardian.co.tt/news/2013-11-25/highway-hit.
2. Kevon Felmine, "Bullet Destroyed Victim's Heart—Autopsy," *T&T Guardian*, November 27, 2013: http://www4.guardian.co.tt/news/2013-11-27/bullet-destroyed-victim%E2%80%99s-heart%E2%80%94autopsy.
3. See "Probe on into Double Slaying," *T&T Newsday*, November 26, 2013: https://archives.newsday.co.tt/2013/11/26/probe-on-into-double-slaying/.
4. Vashtee Achibar, "2 Gunned Down," *T&T Newsday*, November 25, 2013.
5. "Man in Court for a Bullet," *T&T Newsday*, December 3, 2013: http://archives.newsday.co.tt/2013/12/03/man-in-court-for-a-bullet/.
6. Donstan Bonn, "Central Is Now the Murder Capital of T&T," *T&T Express*, April 27, 2018: https://www.trinidadexpress.com/news/local/central-is-now-the-murder-capital-of-t-t/article_c420eb9a-4a42-11e8-b583-57f1da5214fd.html.
7. Derek Achong, "If State Fails to Lay Charges Today … Detained 16 Will Walk," *T&T Guardian*, December 5, 2011: http://www4.guardian.co.tt/news/2011/12/05/if-state-fails-lay-charges-today-detained-16-will-walk.
8. In September 2016, as ISIS was preparing for the loss of the town of Dabiq in northern Syria, the group renamed the magazine "Rumiyah," which is the Arabic name for Rome. The quotation at the beginning of this book is taken from one of the issues of this magazine.
9. "Interview: Abu Sa'd at-Trinidadi," *Dabiq 15*, July 31, 2016: https://azelin.files.wordpress.com/2016/07/the-islamic-state-e2809cdacc84biq-magazine-1522.pdf, p. 66.
10. Ibid.
11. Gail Alexander, "Serious Threat to T&T," *T&T Guardian*, April 16, 2016: http://www.guardian.co.tt/article-6.2.353087.556c49febb.
12. Martin Amis, *Visiting Mrs. Nabokov and Other Excursions* (New York: Random House, 1993), p. 71.

13  Ibid., p. 72.
14  https://www.osac.gov/Pages/ContentReportDetails.aspx?cid=19522.
15  http://cso.gov.tt/.
16  See "Islam in Trinidad and Tobago," in John L. Esposito (ed.), *The Oxford Dictionary of Islam*, http://www.oxfordislamicstudies.com/article/opr/t125/e2400?_hi=0&_pos=14.
17  See "Religious Composition by Country, 2010-2050," *Pew*, April 2, 2015: https://www.pewforum.org/2015/04/02/religious-projection-table/.
18  John McCoy and W. Andy Knight, "Homegrown Violent Extremism in Trinidad and Tobago: Local Patterns, Global Trends," *Studies in Conflict & Terrorism* 40 (4) (2017), p. 14.
19  See esp. Ramesh Deosaran, *A Society under Siege* (St. Augustine: University of the West Indies Press, 1997).
20  Nalinee Seelal, "WPC to Wear Blue Hijab Uniform," *T&T Newsday*, November 12, 2018: https://newsday.co.tt/2018/11/12/wpc-to-wear-blue-hijab-uniform/.
21  Seventeen 13-year-old girls were legally married in T&T in 2010 (see "Child Marriage in Trinidad and Tobago under Spotlight," The Borgen Project, February 23, 2017: https://borgenproject.org/child-marriage-in-trinidad-and-tobago/).

# Chapter 1

1  "Interview: Abu Saʿd at-Trinidadi," p. 65.
2  Ibid., p. 69.
3  According to the national census conducted in 2011, East Indians and Africans are the largest ethnic groups at 35.4 percent and 34.2 percent, respectively; more than 22 percent of the population is identified as "mixed" (Ministry of Planning and Sustainable Development, "Trinidad and Tobago 2011 Population and Housing Census Demographic Report" (Port-of-Spain: Government of the Republic of Trinidad and Tobago, 2011), http://www.tt.undp.org/content/trinidad_tobago/en/home/library/crisis_prevention_and_recovery/publication_1.html, p. 15). Muslims represent about 8 percent of the population (see "Islam in Trinidad and Tobago").

4   "Interview: Abu Sa'd at-Trinidadi," p. 69.
5   Amandla Thomas-Johnson, "US Kills Trinidadian IS Fighter, Then Adds Him to Terrorism List," *Middle East Eye*, April 20, 2017: https://www.middleeasteye.net/news/trinidadian-stuck-us-terror-list-was-already-dead-1297294112.
6   https://www.state.gov/j/ct/rls/other/des/143210.htm.
7   See "Kareem Ibrahim Sentenced to Life in Prison for Conspiring to Commit Terrorist Attack at JFK Airport," U.S. Attorney's Office, January 13, 2012: https://archives.fbi.gov/archives/newyork/press-releases/2012/kareem-ibrahim-sentenced-to-life-in-prison-for-conspiring-to-commit-terrorist-attack-at-jfk-airport.
8   Asha Javeed, "I'm No Isis Point Man," *T&T Sunday Express*, October 17, 2014: https://www.trinidadexpress.com/news/local/i-m-no-isis-point-man/article_f81e3a04-ab5d-5629-b83c-7cb89341e340.html.
9   Derek Achong, "Imam Knocks Police Intel," *T&T Guardian*, February 16, 2018: http://www4.guardian.co.tt/news/2018-02-15/imam-knocks-police-intel.
10  Hannah Arendt, *Eichmann in Jerusalem: A Report on the Banality of Evil* (New York: Viking Press, 1963).
11  See "Clip #4306 WARNING: EXTREMELY GRAPHIC - ISIS TERRORISTS IN SYRIA PLAY WITH DECAPITATED HEAD," MEMRI, June 15, 2014: https://www.memri.org/tv/warning-extremely-graphic-isis-terrorists-syria-play-decapitated-head.
12  Mark Fraser, "Why My Son Fights with ISIS," *T&T Express*, October 10, 2014: https://www.trinidadexpress.com/news/local/why-my-son-fights-with-isis/article_606e2327-546e-5658-ac31-35b0e1db43fa.html.
13  Gail Alexander, "Govt to Meet Muslims on Isis," *T&T Guardian*, August 7, 2016: http://www.guardian.co.tt/article-6.2.356748.5fbef93c56.
14  Derek Achong, "Goat Farmer Denied Bail on Ammo Charges," *T&T Guardian*, September 20, 2011: http://ftp.guardian.co.tt/news/2011/09/20/goat-farmer-denied-bail-ammo-charges.
15  See Derek Achong, "If State Fails to Lay Charges Today … Detained 16 Will Walk," *T&T Guardian*, December 4, 2011: http://www.guardian.co.tt/news/if-state-fails-lay-charges-today-detained-16-will-walk-6.2.456063.9bb10f863a; and Nalinee Seelal, "Sixteen 'Plotters' to Be Freed," *T&T Newsday*, December 5, 2011: https://archives.newsday.co.tt/2011/12/05/sixteen-plotters-to-be-freed/.

16  Fraser, "Why My Son Fights with ISIS."
17  "It's Religious Persecution against Muslims," *T&T Daily Express*, December 7, 2011: https://www.trinidadexpress.com/news/local/it-s-religious-persecution-against-muslims/article_4864eed1-c96b-5c94-9348-542b71e33392.html.
18  "Interview: Abu Sa'd at-Trinidadi," p. 66.
19  Marc Sageman, *Leaderless Jihad: Terror Networks in the Twenty-First Century* (Philadelphia: University of Pennsylvania Press, 2008).
20  "Interview: Abu Sa'd at-Trinidadi," p. 69.
21  Ibid., p.65.
22  Ibid., p. 68.
23  Ibid.
24  Ibid., pp. 68, 69.
25  Ibid., p. 66.
26  Ibid., p. 66.
27  Miranda La Rose, "Dad Calls ISIS Son's Death 'Happiness'," *T&T Newsday*, August 24, 2016: https://archives.newsday.co.tt/2016/08/24/dad-calls-isis-sons-death-happiness/.
28  Frances Robles, "Trying to Stanch Trinidad's Flow of Young Recruits to ISIS," *New York Times*, February 21, 2017: https://www.nytimes.com/2017/02/21/world/americas/trying-to-stanch-trinidads-flow-of-young-recruits-to-isis.html.
29  See "MEDIA RELEASE: LISTING OF SHANE CRAWFORD UNDER THE UNITED NATIONS 1267 ISIL (DA'ESH) & AL-QAIDA SANCTIONS LIST," August 19, 2017: http://www.ag.gov.tt/Portals/0/Documents/AntiTerrorism/Media%20Release.pdf.
30  "Interview: Abu Sa'd at-Trinidadi," p.65.
31  See Simon Cottee, *The Apostates: When Muslims Leave Islam* (London: C. Hurst & Co., 2015).

# Chapter 2

1  Raoul A. Pantin, *Days of Wrath: The 1990 Coup in Trinidad and Tobago* (Lincoln, NE: iUniverse, 2007) p. 17.
2  Ibid., p. 15.

3   Ibid., p. 23.
4   Ibid.
5   Ibid.
6   Alberto M. Fernandez, "Here to Stay and Growing: Combating ISIS Propaganda Networks," The Brookings Project on U.S. Relations with the Islamic World U.S.-Islamic World Forum Papers, October 2015: https://www.brookings.edu/wp-content/uploads/2016/06/IS-Propaganda_Web_English.pdf.
7   Pantin, *Days of Wrath*, p. 17.
8   See https://www.youtube.com/watch?v=xybbUbxHOK4.
9   Selwyn Ryan, *The Muslimeen Grab for Power: Race, Religion and Revolution in Trinidad and Tobago* (Port of Spain: Inprint Caribbean, 1991), p. 52.
10  Williams served as the first post-independence prime minister of T&T from 1962 until his death in 1981. According to Pantin, Williams, an Oxford graduate with a PhD in history, "mesmerized Trinidadians, black Trinidadians in particular, with his scholarship and his fierce anti-colonial rhetoric" (Pantin, *Days of Wrath*, p. 19).
11  Quoted in Deosaran, *A Society under Siege*, p. 66.
12  Pantin, *Days of Wrath*, p. 19.
13  Ibid.
14  Ryan, *The Muslimeen Grab for Power*, p. 53.
15  Estimates of property damage ranged from TT $150 million to $350 million (Deosaran, *A Society under Siege*, p. 19).
16  Ibid., p. 35; Ryan, *The Muslimeen Grab for Power*, p. 274.
17  Ibid., p. 81.
18  See Ryan, *The Muslimeen Grab for Power*, pp. 87–8.
19  Cited in Daurius Figueira, *Jihad in Trinidad and Tobago, July 27, 1990* (Lincoln, NE: Writers Club Press, 2002), p. 18.
20  Pantin, *Days of Wrath*, p. 26.
21  Ibid., p. 27.
22  Ryan, *The Muslimeen Grab for Power*, p. 54.
23  Pantin, *Days of Wrath*, p. 27.
24  Ibid.
25  Ibid.
26  Ibid., p. 29.

27  Ibid., p. 30.
28  Ryan, *The Muslimeen Grab for Power*, p. 316.
29  See esp. Deosaran, *A Society under Siege*, p. 60.
30  Ibid., p. 79.
31  Ibid., p. 80.
32  Pantin, *Days of Wrath*, p. 12.
33  Ibid., p. 13; Deosaran, *A Society under Siege*, pp. 180–1.
34  Deosaran, *A Society under Siege*, p. 81.
35  Quoted in ibid., p. 182.
36  Ibid., p. 126.
37  Quoted in ibid., p. 185.
38  Quoted in ibid., p. 76.
39  Pantin, *Days of Wrath*, p. 43.
40  See esp. Figueira, *Jihad in Trinidad and Tobago, July 27, 1990*, p. 159.
41  Deosaran, *A Society under Siege*, p. 79.
42  Pantin, *Days of Wrath*, p. 153.
43  Quoted in Deosaran, *A Society under Siege*, p. 77.
44  Ibid., pp. 19–20.
45  Pantin, *Days of Wrath*, p. 153.
46  Yvonne Baboolal, "Auctioning of Bakr's Property," *T&T Guardian*, July 25, 2010: http://www.guardian.co.tt/article-6.2.339257.f2a4e5a9a4.
47  Gail Alexander, "Bakr Family Buys Back Two Prime Properties," *T&T Guardian*, August 17, 2010: http://www.guardian.co.tt/news/bakr-family-buys-back-two-prime-properties-6.2.340696.dc09a17815.
48  Quoted in Cynthia Mahabir, "Allah's Outlaws: The Jamaat al Muslimeen of Trinidad and Tobago," *British Journal of Criminology* 53 (2012), p. 68.
49  Gail Alexander, "Bakr Charged with Murder Again," *T&T Guardian*, September 30, 2010: http://www.guardian.co.tt/article-6.2.343244.b9ea0b1a0a.
50  See "Defence Contends Political Motivation at Abu Bakr Trial," *Jamaica Observer*, June 23, 2012: http://www.jamaicaobserver.com/news/Defence-contends-political-motivation-at-Abu-Bakr-trial_11783794.
51  Chris Zambelis, "Jamaat al-Muslimeen: The Growth and Decline of Islamist Militancy in Trinidad and Tobago," *Terrorism Monitor* 7 (23), July 30, 2009: https://jamestown.org/program/jamaat-al-muslimeen-the-growth-and-decline-of-islamist-militancy-in-trinidad-and-tobago/.

52. See "Kareem Ibrahim Sentenced to Life in Prison for Conspiring to Commit Terrorist Attack at JFK Airport."
53. Derek Achong, "Yasin Abu Bakr and Hassan Ali Released without Charge," *T&T Guardian*, July 21, 2015: http://guardian.co.tt/news/yasin-abu-bakr-and-hassan-ali-released-without-charge-6.2.367130.db1000b31f.
54. Danny Gold, "The Islamic Leader Who Tried to Overthrow Trinidad Has Mellowed … a Little," *Vice*, May 30, 2014: https://news.vice.com/en_us/article/yw4e3m/the-islamic-leader-who-tried-to-overthrow-trinidad-has-mellowed-a-little.
55. Pantin, *Days of Wrath*, p. 53.
56. Ibid.
57. Ibid., p. 138.
58. Ibid.
59. See "Leader of the Jamaat al Muslimeen Proclaims Support for US President, Donald Trump," Power 102FM, February 7, 2017: https://news.power102fm.com/leader-of-the-jamaat-al-muslimeen-proclaims-support-for-u-s-president-donald-trump-43109.
60. Mahabir, "Allah's Outlaws," p. 61.
61. Ibid.
62. Ibid.

# Chapter 3

1. See https://jihadology.net/2014/08/02/al-%E1%B8%A5ayat-media-center-presents-a-new-video-message-from-the-islamic-state-id-greetings-from-the-land-of-the-caliphate/.
2. See https://jihadology.net/2017/11/29/new-video-message-from-the-islamic-state-flames-of-war-ii//.
3. See https://vimeo.com/ondemand/insideis.
4. Josie Ensor, "Foreign Wives and Widows Face Conveyor-belt Justice in Iraqi Courts after the Defeat of Islamic State," *The Telegraph*, May 1, 2018: https://www.telegraph.co.uk/news/2018/05/01/islamic-state-wives-widows-face-reckoning-iraqi-courts/.
5. Alexander, "Serious threat to T&T."

6   Jensen La Vende, "I Want to Come Home," *T&T Newsday*, November 26, 2018: https://newsday.co.tt/2018/11/26/i-want-to-come-home/.
7   Martin Chulov, "Losing Ground, Fighters and Morale – Is It All over for Isis?," *The Guardian*, September 7, 2016: https://www.theguardian.com/world/2016/sep/07/losing-ground-fighter-morale-is-it-all-over-for-isis-syria-turkey.
8   Denise Balgobin, "Tariq Abdul-Haqq—the Schoolboy Gladiator," *T&T Newsday*, August 16, 2007: https://archives.newsday.co.tt/2007/08/16/tariq-abdul-haqq-the-schoolboy-gladiator/.
9   McCoy and Knight, "Homegrown Violent Extremism in Trinidad and Tobago."
10  Joana Cook and Gina Vale, "From Daesh to 'Diaspora,'" ICSR, 2018: https://icsr.info/wp-content/uploads/2018/07/Women-in-ISIS-report_20180719_web.pdf.
11  The Soufan Group, "Foreign Fighters: An Updated Assessment," December 2, 2015: http://soufangroup.com/wp-content/uploads/2015/12/TSG_ForeignFightersUpdate3.pdf, p. 4.
12  McCoy and Knight, "Homegrown Violent Extremism in Trinidad and Tobago," pp. 13–14.
13  Sageman, *Leaderless Jihad*, pp. 47–8.
14  See Martha Crenshaw, "The Causes of Terrorism," *Comparative Politics* 13 (4) (1981), p. 390; Andrew Silke, "Cheshire- Cat Logic: The Recurring Theme of Terrorist Abnormality in Psychological Research," *Psychology, Crime & Law* 4 (1) (1998), pp. 51–69; Randy Borum, *Psychology of Terrorism* (Tampa: University of South Florida, 2004), p. 32.
15  Simon Cottee and Keith Hayward Terrorist (E)motives: The Existential Attractions of Terrorism, *Studies in Conflict & Terrorism* 34 (12) (2011), p. 963.
16  Graeme Wood, "The Three Types of People Who Fight for ISIS," *The New Republic*, September 11, 2014: https://newrepublic.com/article/119395/isiss-three-types-fighters.
17  Bibi van Ginkel and Eva Entenmann, *The Foreign Fighters Phenomenon in the European Union: Profiles, Threats and Policies*, ICCT Research Paper (The Hague: International Centre for Counter-Terrorism, April 2016): https://www.icct.nl/wp-content/uploads/2016/03/ICCT-Report_Foreign-Fighters-Phenomenon-in-the-EU_1-April-2016_including-AnnexesLinks.pdf, p. 40.

18 Daniel H. Heinke and Jan Raudszus, "German Foreign Fighters in Syria and Iraq," *CTC Sentinel* 8 (1) (January 2015): https://ctc.usma.edu/german-foreign-fighters-in-syria-and-iraq/, p. 19.
19 Linus Gustafsson and Magnus Ranstorp, *Swedish Foreign Fighters in Syria and Iraq: An Analysis of Open-source Intelligence and Statistical Data* (Stockholm: Swedish Defence University, 2017): https://www.diva-portal.org/smash/get/diva2:1110355/FULLTEXT01.pdf, pp. 5, 80.
20 Edwin Bakker and Roel de Bont, "Belgian and Dutch jihadist foreign fighters (2012–2015): Characteristics, Motivations, and Roles in the War in Syria and Iraq," *Small Wars and Insurgencies* 27 (5) (2016), p. 841.
21 Ibid.
22 Meleagrou-Hitchens et al., *The Travelers*, Alexander Meleagrou-Hitchens, Seamus Hughes and Bennett Clifford, *The Travelers: American jihadists in Syria and Iraq* (Washington, DC: George Washington University, Program on Extremism (February 2018): https://extremism.gwu.edu/sites/g/files/zaxdzs2191/f/TravelersAmericanJihadistsinSyriaandIraq.pdf, p. 17.
23 See esp. Olivier Roy, *Jihad and Death: The Global appeal of Islamic State* (London: Hurst, 2017), p. 2; Rik Coolsaet, *Facing the Fourth Foreign Fighter Wave: What Drives Europeans to Syria, and to Islamic State? Insights from the Belgian Case*, Egmont Paper no. 81 (Brussels: Royal Institute for International Relations, March 2016): http://www.egmontinstitute.be/content/uploads/2016/02/egmont.papers.81_online-versie.pdf?type=pdf, p. 36.
24 See esp. Aaron Zelin, "ISIS Is Dead, Long Live the Islamic State," *Foreign Policy*, June 30, 2014: http://foreignpolicy.com/2014/06/30/isis-is-dead-long-live-the-islamic-state/.
25 See data presented in *Trading Economics*, https://tradingeconomics.com/trinidad-and-tobago/barro-lee-percentage-of-population-age-30-34-with-secondary-schooling-completed-secondary-wb-data.html.
26 See Oxford Business Group, *Trinidad and Tobago's Education System Is Multi-Faceted and Well-Funded* (Oxford, 2015): https://oxfordbusinessgroup.com/overview/trinidad-and-tobagos-education-system-multi-faceted-and-well-funded.
27 The distinction is based on the World Bank's definition of "class," according to which the middle-class income bracket in Latin America and the Caribbean is US$10–US$50 per capita per day. See Francisco

H. G. Ferreira, Julian Messina, Jamele Rigolini, Luis-Felipe López-Calva, Maria Ana Lugo and Renos Vakis, *Economic Mobility and the Rise of the Latin American Middle Class* (Washington, DC: World Bank, 2013): https://openknowledge.worldbank.org/bitstream/handle/10986/11858/9780821396346.pdf?sequence=, p. 2.

28 "Interview: Abu Sa'd at-Trinidadi," p. 68.
29 Bart Schuurman, Peter Grol, and Scott Flower, *Converts and Islamist Terrorism: An Introduction*, ICCT Policy Brief (The Hague: International Centre for Counter-Terrorism, June 2016): https://www.icctnl/wp-content/uploads/2016/06/ICCT-Schuurman-Grol-Flower-Converts-June-2016.pdf.
30 Van Ginkel and Entenmann, *The Foreign Fighters Phenomenon in the European Union*, pp. 4, 52.
31 This number is calculated on the basis of the estimates provided in McCoy and Knight, "Homegrown Violent Extremism in Trinidad and Tobago," p. 272.
32 See Simon Cottee, "Reborn into Terrorism," *The Atlantic*, January 25, 2016: https://www.theatlantic.com/international/archive/2016/01/isis-criminals-converts/426822/.
33 Bakker and de Bont, "Belgian and Dutch jihadist Foreign Fighters (2012–2015)," p. 844.
34 Gustafsson and Ranstorp, *Swedish Foreign Fighters in Syria and Iraq*, p. 71.
35 Ibid.
36 See Sean C. Reynolds and Mohammed M. Hafez, "Social Network Analysis of German Foreign Fighters in Syria and Iraq," *Terrorism and Political Violence* 31 (4) (2019).
37 For a particularly vivid statement of this point, see Graeme Wood, *The Way of the Strangers: Encounters with the Islamic State* (London: Penguin, 2017), pp. 91–9.
38 See esp. Amir Rostami, Joakim Sturup, Hernan Mondani, Pia Thevselius, Jerzy Sarnecki, and Christofer Edling, "The Swedish *mujahideen*: An Exploratory Study of 41 Swedish Foreign Fighters Deceased in Iraq and Syria," *Studies in Conflict and Terrorism*, 2018, p. 3; Bakker and de Bont, "Belgian and Dutch jihadist foreign fighters (2012–2015)," pp. 840–3; and Reynolds and Hafez, "Social Network Analysis of German Foreign Fighters in Syria and Iraq," pp. 8–12.

39  See Scott Atran, "Youth, Violent Extremism and Promoting Peace," PLOS blogs, 25 April 2015: https://blogs.plos.org/neuroanthropology/2015/04/25/scott-atran-on-youth-violent-extremism-and-promoting-peace/.
40  See esp. Lorne L. Dawson and Amarnath Amarasingam, "Talking to Foreign Fighters," *Studies in Conflict & Terrorism* 40 (3) (2017), pp. 191–210.
41  This was broadcast on a major TV news show in Trinidad in May 2014: https://www.tv6tnt.com/news/7pmnews/mark-bassant-investigates-jihadists-among-us/article_94c1c235-1822-5680-a143-8b7515e1ac13.html.
42  "ISIS Pays Foreign Fighters $1,000 a Month: Jordan King," NBC News, September 22, 2014: https://www.nbcnews.com/storyline/isis-terror/isis-pays-foreign-fighters-1-000-month-jordan-king-n209026.
43  Carla E. Humud, Robert Pirog, and Liana Rosen, "Islamic State Financing and U.S. Policy Approaches," *Congressional Research Service*, April 10, 2015: https://fas.org/sgp/crs/terror/R43980.pdf, p. 13.
44  Max Weber, *Economy and Society* (Berkeley: University of California Press, 1978), p. 23.
45  Quoted in: "Exclusive Interview from Inside IS-detention Center, A Caribbean ISIS Mechanic," North-Press Agency Al-Hasakah – Northeastern Syria, June 18, 2019: https://npasyria.com/en/blog.php?id_blog=265&sub_blog=4%20&name_blog=Exclusive%20interview%20from%20inside%20IS-detention%20Center,%20A%20Caribbean%20ISIS%20mechanic.
46  See https://jihadology.net/2015/11/05/new-video-message-from-the-islamic-state-those-who-have-believed-and-emigrated-wilayat-al-raqqah/.
47  See Adam Goldman and Scott Shane, "A Long-Pursued ISIS Preacher Is Finally Charged in New York," *New York Times*, September 1, 2017: https://www.nytimes.com/2017/09/01/us/abdullah-faisal-al-qaeda.html. El-Faisal is also believed to have acted as a mentor to the Jamaican-born British national Jermaine Lindsay, who detonated a bomb on a Tube train near King's Cross, killing twenty-six passengers, in the July 7, 2005, London bombings ("Profile: Germaine Lindsay," *BBC News*, March 2, 2011: http://www.bbc.co.uk/news/uk-12621385).
48  Shaliza Hassanali, "Man Held in Plot to Assassinate PM, Cabinet Members Running Scared," *T&T Guardian*, December 11, 2011: http://

www4.guardian.co.tt/news/2011/12/11/man-held-plot-assassinate-pm-cabinet-membersrunning-scared.

49  Ibid.
50  See Christopher Hitchens, "On the Frontier of Apocalypse," *Vanity Fair*, January, 2002: https://www.vanityfair.com/news/2002/01/pakistan-200201.
51  Rukmini Callimachi, "American ISIS Member Caught on Syrian Battlefield, Militia Says," *The New York Times*, January 6, 2019: https://www.nytimes.com/2019/01/06/world/middleeast/isis-syria-warren-christopher-clark.html.
52  It was initially believed, based on his *kunya*, that Parson was an American: see, for example, Lorenzo Vidino and Seamus Hughes, "ISIS in America: From Retweets to Raqqa," Program on Extremism, December 2015: https://extremism.gwu.edu/sites/g/files/zaxdzs2191/f/downloads/ISIS%20in%20America%20-%20Full%20Report.pdf, pp. 12–13.
53  Adam Goldman and Eric Schmitt, "One by One, ISIS Social Media Experts Are Killed as Result of F.B.I. Program," *New York Times*, November 24, 2016: https://www.nytimes.com/2016/11/24/world/middleeast/isis-recruiters-social-media.html?mtrref=undefined&login=email; Alexander Meleagrou-Hitchens and Seamus Hughes, "The Threat to the United States from the Islamic State's Virtual Entrepreneurs," *CTC Sentinel*, March 2017, 10 (3): https://ctc.usma.edu/the-threat-to-the-united-states-from-the-islamic-states-virtual-entrepreneurs/.
54  See https://ismailabduljabbaralbrazili.wordpress.com/tag/abu-khalid-al-amriki/.
55  https://extremism.gwu.edu/sites/g/files/zaxdzs2191/f/ThomasGovernmentSentencingMemo.pdf, p. 2.
56  Ibid., p. 3. This was on February 17, 2015.
57  Ibid.
58  http://media.philly.com/documents/KeonnaThomasComplaint.pdf, p. 5.
59  Jeremy Roebuck, "North Philly Woman Gets 8-year Term for Plan to Leave Kids, Marry ISIS Soldier," *The Inquirer*, September 6, 2017: http://www.philly.com/philly/news/pennsylvania/philadelphia/north-philly-mom-gets-8-year-term-for-plan-to-leave-kids-marry-isis-soldier-20170906.html; Scott Calvert and Andrew Grossman, "Philadelphia Woman Keonna Thomas Charged with Attempting to Join

ISIS," *The Wall Street Journal*, April 3, 2015: https://www.wsj.com/articles/philadelphia-woman-keonna-thomas-charged-with-attempting-to-join-isis-1428078216.

60 See Jeremy Roebuck, "Facing Sentencing, N. Philly Mom Married to Islamic State Soldier Is No Aberration," *The Inquirer*, September 4, 2017: http://www.philly.com/philly/news/pennsylvania/philadelphia/facing-sentencing-n-philly-mom-married-to-isis-soldier-is-no-aberration-20170905.html; http://media.philly.com/documents/KeonnaThomasComplaint.pdf, p. 4.

61 Lauren Williams, "Meeting a Daesh jihadist in Syria," *The Saturday Paper*, July 18, 2015: https://www.thesaturdaypaper.com.au/world/2015/07/18/meeting-daesh-jihadist-syria/14371416002139.

62 Ibid.

63 See "American IS Fighter Purportedly Killed in Syria According to Twitter Accounts," SITE, September, 17, 2015: https://news.siteintelgroup.com/Western-Jihadist-Forum-Digest/american-is-fighter-purportedly-killed-in-syria-according-to-twitter-accounts.html; see also: https://twitter.com/gwupoe/status/644893435246346241?lang=en.

64 Quoted in Lorenzo Vidino and Seamus Hughes, "ISIS in America: From Retweets to Raqqa," p. 14.

65 John Horgan, "Don't Ask Why People Join the Islamic State— Ask How," *Vice*, September 10, 2014: https://www.vice.com/en_us/article/wjyygy/dont-ask-why-people-join-the-islamic-state-ask-how.

66 See "Treasury Sanctions Key ISIS Financial Facilitators," September 19, 2018: https://home.treasury.gov/news/press-releases/sm489.

67 Javeed, "I'm No Isis Point Man."

68 Ismail Khan, "Pakistani Military Kills a Qaeda Leader," *New York Times*, December 6, 2014: https://www.nytimes.com/2014/12/07/world/pakistan-kills-senior-qaeda-leader-wanted-by-fbi.html.

69 "Terror Suspect Has Close Links to Caribbean; FBI Keeps Tabs on Trini Friends," *T&T Guardian*, May 28, 2004: http://www.freerepublic.com/focus/f-news/1144256/posts.

70 Mahabir, "Allah's Outlaws," pp. 59–73.

71 Chris Zambelis, "Jamaat al-Muslimeen: The Growth and Decline of Islamist Militancy in Trinidad and Tobago," *Terrorism Monitor* 7 (23): July 30, 2009: https://jamestown.org/program/jamaat-al-muslimeen-the-growth-and-decline-of-islamist-militancy-in-trinidad-and-tobago/.

## Chapter 4

1. See Khaled al-Ramahi and Maher Chmaytelli, "Iraq Declares End of Caliphate after Capture of Mosul Mosque," Reuters, June 29, 2017: https://www.reuters.com/article/us-mideast-crisis-iraq-mosul-idUSKBN19K0YZ.
2. Quoted in Ensor, "Foreign Wives and Widows Face Conveyor-belt Justice in Iraqi Courts after the Defeat of Islamic State."
3. Quoted in Zelin, "ISIS Is Dead, Long Live the Islamic State."
4. Ibid.
5. Ensor, "Foreign Wives and Widows Face Conveyor-belt Justice in Iraqi Courts after the Defeat of Islamic State."
6. Azard Ali, "'We Want to Come Home,'" *T&T Newsday*, May 17, 2018: https://newsday.co.tt/2018/05/17/we-want-to-come-home/
7. Shaliza Hassanali, "Imam Defends Name over Isis Allegations: I Don't Know Crawford," *T&T Guardian*, August 8, 2016: http://www.tobagotoday.co.tt/news/2016-08-08/imam-defends-name-over-isis-allegations-i-don%E2%80%99t-know-crawford.
8. Pantin, *Days of Wrath*, p. 46.
9. Ibid., p. 47.
10. Ibid.
11. Thomas Hegghammer, "Terrorist Recruitment and Radicalisation in Saudi Arabia," *Middle East Policy* 13 (4) (2006), p. 50.
12. See "Shot Mayaro Man Dies at Hospital," *T&T Guardian*, February 7, 2010: http://www.guardian.co.tt/article-6.2.328893.f5fe5c71ef.
13. Ragoonath and Boodan, "Highway Hit."
14. Javeed, "I'm No Isis Point Man."

## Chapter 5

1. See Deosaran, A *Society under Siege*, p. 258.
2. See, for example, https://twitter.com/Sh_1d_0w/status/726502080949682176.
3. See "Department of Defense Press Briefing by Pentagon Press Secretary Peter Cook in the Pentagon Briefing Room," May 5, 2016: https://

dod.defense.gov/News/Transcripts/Transcript-View/Article/752789/department-of-defense-press-briefing-by-pentagon-press-secretary-peter-cook-in/.

4   It wasn't until February 2017 that the Pentagon ditched this habit: see Ryan Browne, "Trump Pentagon Names the Enemy: It's ISIS, Not ISIL," *CNN*, February 25, 2017: https://edition.cnn.com/2017/02/24/politics/isis-isil-name-change-trump/index.html.

5   Emma Partridge, "Curtis Cheng Murder: Shadi Jabar, Sister of Parramatta Killer Caught on Camera Bound for Syria," *The Daily Telegraph*, May 4, 2017: https://www.dailytelegraph.com.au/news/nsw/curtis-cheng-murder-shadi-jabar-sister-of-parramatta-killer-caught-on-camera-bound-for-syria/news-story/9f5a5aee3f01daeea561cb8b6f067fc5.

6   Siobhan Fogarty, "NSW Police Headquarters Gunman Identified as Farhad Khalil Mohammad Jabar," *ABC News*, October 3, 2015, 2016: https://www.abc.net.au/news/2015-10-03/nsw-police-headquarters-gunman-named/6825466.

7   Rukmini Callimachi, "Not 'Lone Wolves' After All: How ISIS Guides World's Terror Plots from Afar," *The New York Times*, February 4, 2017: https://www.nytimes.com/2017/02/04/world/asia/isis-messaging-app-terror-plot.html.

8   On July 6, 2018, Daniels was sentenced to eighty months in prison for attempting to provide material support to ISIS: see "Columbus Man Sentenced to 80 Months in Prison for Attempting to Provide Material Support to ISIS," Department of Justice, July 6, 2018: https://www.justice.gov/usao-sdoh/pr/columbus-man-sentenced-80-months-prison-attempting-provide-material-support-isis.

9   https://extremism.gwu.edu/sites/g/files/zaxdzs2191/f/Daniels%20Arrest%20Warrant%2C%20Criminal%20Complaint.pdf, p. 5.

10  See "Ohio Man Arrested for Attempting to Provide Material Support to ISIL," Department of Justice, November 7, 2016: https://www.justice.gov/opa/pr/ohio-man-arrested-attempting-provide-material-support-isil.

11  https://extremism.gwu.edu/sites/g/files/zaxdzs2191/f/Daniels%20Arrest%20Warrant%2C%20Criminal%20Complaint.pdf, p. 7.

12  "Interview: Abu Sa'd at-Trinidadi," pp. 65–6.

13  Ibid., p. 66.

14  Ibid.

15  Ibid., p. 67.
16  Ibid.
17  "Man in Court for a Bullet," *T&T Newsday*.
18  See Achibar, "2 Gunned Down," *T&T Newsday*.
19  "Man in Court for a Bullet."
20  https://www.facebook.com/BeyondTheTape/photos/a.259994307525069.1073741831.240977966093370/319348958256270/?type=3&theater.
21  See Jake Ryan, "ISIS Fiend Wiped Out in Drone Strike after Sun Uncovered Terror Plot to Attack Britain," *The Sun*, May 15, 2016: https://www.thesun.co.uk/archives/news/1178205/isis-fiend-wiped-out-in-drone-strike-after-sun-uncovered-terror-plot-to-attack-britain/.
22  "Interview: Abu Sa'd at-Trinidadi," p.65.
23  "Man in Court for a Bullet."
24  Mark Bassant, "V'zuela Charges 5 Trinis," *T&T Express*, November 13, 2014: https://www.trinidadexpress.com/news/local/vzuela-charges-trinis/article_8ec4458b-ddac-56ee-bee5-aafd330f6e1f.html; McCoy and Knight, "Homegrown Violent Extremism in Trinidad and Tobago," pp. 14–15.
25  This woman was the wife of Milton Algernon: see "50 Trinis Fighting with ISIS Terrorists in Syria," *The T&T Express*, September 24, 2014: https://www.trinidadexpress.com/news/local/trinis-fighting-with-isis-terrorists-in-syria/article_a913631a-f282-5ea9-89a8-8d288364a17c.html; see also Alexander, "Serious Threat to T&T."
26  Griff Witte, Sudarsan Raghavan, and James McAuley, "Flow of Foreign Fighters Plummets as Islamic State Loses Its Edge," *The Washington Post*, September 9, 2016: https://www.washingtonpost.com/world/europe/flow-of-foreign-fighters-plummets-as-isis-loses-its-edge/2016/09/09/ed3e0dda-751b-11e6-9781-49e591781754_story.html?utm_term=.0832d2886476.
27  See "Country Reports on Terrorism 2016," United States Department of State Publication, July 2017: https://www.state.gov/documents/organization/272488.pdf, p. 300.
28  See "Country Reports on Terrorism 2017," United States Department of State Publication, September 2018: https://www.state.gov/documents/organization/283100.pdf, p. 214.
29  Jensen La Vende, "Anti-Terrorism Act Now Law," *T&T Newsday*, August 20, 2018: https://newsday.co.tt/2018/08/20/anti-terrorism-act-now-law/.

30  Carolyn Kissoon, "The Anti-Terrorism Bill Is Dead: Kamla Explains Why," *T&T Express*, July 3, 2018: https://www.trinidadexpress.com/news/local/the-anti-terrorism-bill-is-dead-kamla-explains-why/article_47c1228e-7ec9-11e8-a919-b7061680edef.html.
31  Rhondor Dowlat, "New Offence Proposed for Anti-Terror Bill," *T&T Guardian*, April 28, 2018: http://ftp.guardian.co.tt/news/2018-04-28/new-offence-proposed-anti-terror-bill.
32  See http://www.ttparliament.org/reports/p11-s3-J-20180605-TERRrFinal.pdf, p. 57.
33  Gail Alexander, "Five Trinis Held in Venezuela Set Free," *T&T Guardian*: October 15, 2016: http://www.guardian.co.tt/news/five-trinis-held-venezuela-set-free-6.2.359035.2ca2d78127.
34  Gail Alexander, "Nafeesa Defends Relative of Muslim Returnee Wearing 'Isis' Jacket," *T&T Guardian*, November 27, 2016:http://ftp.guardian.co.tt/news/2016-11-27/nafeesa-defends-relative-muslim-returnee-wearing-%E2%80%98isis%E2%80%99-jacket.
35  See, for example, Robles, "Trying to Stanch Trinidad's Flow of Young Recruits to ISIS"; Muhammad Fraser-Rahim, "How We Can Stop Isis in the Caribbean?," *Newsweek*, February 13, 2018: https://www.newsweek.com/how-we-can-stop-isis-caribbean-804492; "Caribbean to Caliphate," Aljazeera, May 17, 2017: https://www.aljazeera.com/programmes/peopleandpower/2017/05/caribbean-caliphate-170517073332147.html; and https://www.cnc3.co.tt/news/national-geographic-highlights-tts-isis-connections.
36  Quoted in Emma Graham-Harrison and Joshua Surtees, "Trinidad's Jihadis: How Tiny Nation Became Isis Recruiting Ground," *The Guardian*, February 2, 2018: https://www.theguardian.com/world/2018/feb/02/trinidad-jihadis-isis-tobago-tariq-abdul-haqq.
37  Ibid.
38  http://www.ttparliament.org/hansards/hh20170526.pdf, p. 20.
39  Ibid., p. 28.
40  Ibid., p. 31.
41  Ibid.
42  Simon Cottee, "ISIS in the Caribbean," *The Atlantic*, December 8, 2016: https://www.theatlantic.com/international/archive/2016/12/isis-trinidad/509930/.
43  http://www.ttparliament.org/hansards/hh20170526.pdf, p. 33.

44  Ibid., p.32.
45  Ibid., pp. 43–4.
46  Ibid., p. 78.
47  Ibid.
48  Ibid., p. 80.
49  Alexander, "Serious Threat to T&T."
50  See http://www.ttparliament.org/legislations/b2016h05.pdf.
51  See Gail Alexander, "Rehab for Radicalized Fighters—Dillon," *T&T Guardian*, November 26, 2017: http://www.tobagotoday.co.tt/news/2017-11-25/rehab-radicalized-fighters%E2%80%94dillon.
52  See Kevon Felmine, "Carli Bay Locked Down as Suspect Drops Grenade to Evade Cops," *T&T Guardian*, May 31, 2016: http://www.guardian.co.tt/article-6.2.354628.ece53b01a7.
53  See "Gary Griffith Appointed Commissioner of Police by PSC," *T&T Express*, August 6, 2018: https://www.trinidadexpress.com/news/local/gary-griffith-appointed-commissioner-of-police-by-psc/article_71a441d8-9988-11e8-938c-a321b5ea6afe.html.
54  Alexander Bruzual, "Griffith: No Honeymoon Period for Me," *T&T Express*, August 17, 2018: https://www.trinidadexpress.com/news/local/griffith-no-honeymoon-period-for-me/article_026fdbea-a245-11e8-8f1a-57950a9b404c.html.
55  Jensen La Vende, "Gary on the Beat: CoP on the Frontline with Rank and File," *T&T Newsday*, August 26, 2018, https://newsday.co.tt/2018/08/26/gary-on-the-beat/.
56  Darlisa Ghouralal, "Gary on Camo Kit Critics," *T&T Loop*, February 21, 2019: http://www.looptt.com/content/gary-camo-kit-critics-let-them-focus-what-i-wear.
57  Tom Zoellner, "Trinidad Prosecutor Dana Seetahal's Gangland Murder Goes Unpunished," *New Times Broward-Palm Beach*, March 1, 2016: https://www.browardpalmbeach.com/news/trinidad-prosecutor-dana-seetahals-gangland-murder-goes-unpunished-7619482.
58  Dareece Polo, "Four Arrested as Police Reveal Threat to Disrupt Carnival 2018," *The Loop*, February 8, 2018: http://www.looptt.com/content/four-arrested-threat-carnival.
59  Ryan Browne and Barbara Starr, "US Military Helps Thwart Trinidad Carnival Terror Attack," *CNN*, February 9, 2018: https://edition.cnn.com/2018/02/09/politics/trinidad-carnival-terror-attack-thwarted/index.html.

60  Ibid.
61  Ibid.
62  See "Cops Keep Freed Carnival Plot Detainees' Property," *CNC3*, February 18, 2018: https://www.cnc3.co.tt/press-release/cops-keep-freed-carnival-plot-detainees%E2%80%99-property.
63  See "Carnival Deaths: Three Killed in Separate Incidents," *The Loop*, February 12, 2018: http://www.looptt.com/content/carnival-killings-three-dead-separate-incidents.
64  See "Safe Opening," *T&T Guardian*, February 13, 2018: http://jupiter.guardian.co.tt/editorial/2018-02-13/safe-opening.
65  See http://www.planning.gov.tt/content/cso-releases-carnival-2017-visitor-arrivals-and-expenditure.
66  See "Readout of the President's Call with Prime Minister Keith Rowley of Trinidad and Tobago," February 19, 2017: https://www.whitehouse.gov/briefings-statements/readout-presidents-call-prime-minister-keith-rowley-trinidad-tobago/.
67  Robles, "Trying to Staunch Trinidad's Flow of Young Recruits to ISIS."
68  Cited in Joey Millar, "Winter Travel Warning: Terror Threat for British Tourists Visiting Trinidad and Tobago," *The Express*, October 25, 2017: https://www.express.co.uk/news/world/871143/trinidad-tobago-travel-information-terror-threat-uk-tourists
69  Dareece Polo, "Rowley: Carnival Terror Plot 'No Joke'," *The Loop*, February 14, 2018: http://www.looptt.com/content/rowley-carnival-terror-plot-no-joke.
70  Alina Doodnath, "PM Confirms ISIS Cells Active in T&T," *The Loop*, February 16, 2018: http://www.looptt.com/content/pm-confirms-isis-cells-active-tt.
71  Ibid.
72  See "Trinidad Opposition Slams Attorney General's Attempted Denial of Local ISIS Cell," *Caribbean News Now*, February 19, 2018: https://www.caribbeannewsnow.com/2018/02/19/trinidad-opposition-slams-attorney-generals-attempted-denial-local-isis-cell/. See also Carla Bridglal, "Faris Backtracks on ISIS: Says Newsday 'Misunderstood' Comments," *T&T Newsday*, February 20, 2018: https://newsday.co.tt/2018/02/20/faris-backtracks-on-isis-says-newsday-misunderstood-comments/.

## Chapter 6

1. Quoted in Mark Fraser, "Bring Back My Kids," *T&T Express*, December 8, 2014.
2. Quoted in Ben Hubbard, "In a Crowded Syria Tent Camp, the Women and Children of ISIS Wait in Limbo," *The New York Times*, March 29, 2019: https://www.nytimes.com/2019/03/29/world/middleeast/isis-syria-women-children.html.
3. Wladimir van Wilgenburg, "SDF-led Special Forces Arrest Eight Foreign IS Fighters, Including One American," Kurdistan 24, January 9, 2019: http://www.kurdistan24.net/en/news/8ca04e4c-a55d-4dbe-a765-73b3dccee34a.
4. Rukmini Callimachi, "American ISIS Member Caught on Syrian Battlefield," *New York Times*, January 6, 2019: https://www.nytimes.com/2019/01/06/world/middleeast/isis-syria-warren-christopher-clark.html.
5. Richard Engel, "American ISIS Member Warren Clark Says He Wanted to See 'What the Group Was About'," *NBC News*, January 16, 2019: https://www.nbcnews.com/news/world/american-isis-member-detained-syria-says-he-wanted-go-see-n958711.
6. See https://jihadology.net/2015/11/05/new-video-message-from-the-islamic-state-those-who-have-believed-and-emigrated-wilayat-al-raqqah/.
7. Rukmini Callimachi and Eric Schmitt, "Teenager Captured with ISIS Fighters Is from Trinidad, Not the U.S., Officials Say," *New York Times*, January 11, 2019: https://www.nytimes.com/2019/01/11/world/middleeast/teenager-isis-syria-trinidad.html.
8. Ana van Es, "Aan de Eufraat bombarderen Amerikanen de laatste resten van IS naar de vergetelheid—of niet?," *de volkskrant*, January 11, 2019: https://www.volkskrant.nl/kijkverder/v/2019/strijd-om-de-laatste-syrische-dorpen/.
9. Hubbard, "In a Crowded Syria Tent Camp, the Women and Children of ISIS Wait in Limbo."
10. According to an article by Horgan et al., "six pre-adolescent children were eulogized [by ISIS in its propaganda] as suicide bombers, special operations operatives, and regular foot-soldiers between 2015 and

2016" (Horgan et al., "From Cubs to Lions: A Six Stage Model of Child Socialization into the Islamic State," *Studies in Conflict & Terrorism* 40 (7) (2017), p. 653).

11  Rukmini Callimachi, "ISIS Enshrines a Theology of Rape," *The New York Times*, August 13, 2015: https://www.nytimes.com/2015/08/14/world/middleeast/isis-enshrines-a-theology-of-rape.html.

12  See Tim Arango, "A Boy in ISIS. A Suicide Vest. A Hope to Live," *The New York Times*, December 26, 2014: https://www.nytimes.com/2014/12/27/world/middleeast/syria-isis-recruits-teenagers-as-suicide-bombers.html?_r=1.

13  Alexander, "Serious Threat to T&T."

14  See Robin Wright, "The Ignominious End of the ISIS Caliphate," *The New Yorker*, October 2017: https://www.newyorker.com/news/news-desk/the-ignominious-end-of-the-isis-caliphate.

15  See Bethan McKernan and Joshua Surtees, "Trapped in Syria: Children Kidnapped by Isis Who Can't Go Home," *The Guardian*, December 29, 2018:, https://www.theguardian.com/world/2018/dec/29/trapped-in-syria-children-kidnapped-by-isis-who-cant-go-home.

16  Bethan McKernan and Joshua Surtees, "'At last, I Can Sleep': Brothers Kidnapped by Isis Reunited with Mother in Syria," *The Guardian*, January 22, 2019: https://www.theguardian.com/world/2019/jan/22/at-last-i-can-sleep-brothers-kidnapped-by-isis-reunited-with-mother-in-syria.

17  Ibid.

18  See "Trinidadian Mom Reunites with Kids Taken by Their Father to ISIS," *NPR*, January 26, 2019: https://www.npr.org/2019/01/26/688326707/trinidadian-kids-taken-away-to-isis-reunite-with-mom-thanks-to-help-from-a-rock-; Russell Hope, "Pink Floyd Star Uses Private Jet to Reunite Mother with Her Kidnapped Children," *Sky News*, January 23, 2019: https://news.sky.com/story/pink-floyd-star-uses-private-jet-to-reunite-mother-with-her-kidnapped-children-11615181.

19  See "Lawyer on Syria Rescue Mission: No Help from TT Govt," *T&T Newsday*, January 23, 2019: https://newsday.co.tt/2019/01/23/lawyer-on-syria-rescue-mission-no-help-from-tt-govt/.

20  See "Repatriation and Reintegration of T&T Nationals Held in Refugee & Detention Camps in Syria and Iraq," January 22, 2019: http://www.news.gov.tt/content/repatriation-and-reintegration-tt-nationals-held-refugee-detention-camps-syria-and-iraq#.XLh9rOhKjIU.

21  Ibid.
22  McKernan and Surtees, "Trapped in Syria."
23  Julien Neaves, "Mom of Trini Brothers Kept in Syria: Govt Seems Not to Care," *T&T Newsday*, January 4, 2019: https://newsday.co.tt/2019/01/04/mom-of-trini-brothers-kept-in-syria-govt-seems-not-to-care/.
24  "Lawyer on Syria Rescue Mission."
25  Joan Rampersad, "'Wrong to Say We Did Nothing'," *T&T Newsday*, January 24, 2019: https://newsday.co.tt/2019/01/24/wrong-to-say-we-did-nothing/.
26  Ibid.
27  In a 2013 article on the "hottest young talent in the Pro League this season," posted on the Socca Warriors.net website, Nuru Mohammed is described as: "Tall, strong and quick over the first few metres … a sturdy central defender. Not flashy but capable of getting the job done." (This article is no longer available.)
28  John Sparks, "IS brides' Utopian Fantasy Has Ended in De Facto Imprisonment," *Sky News*, February 25, 2019: https://news.sky.com/story/islamic-state-women-begging-for-food-and-medicine-in-syria-camp-11644249.
29  Gail Alexander, "Muslim Body: 40 Locals from Isis Need to Come Home," *T&T Guardian*, July 3, 2019: https://www.guardian.co.tt/news/muslim-body-40-locals-from-isis-need-to-come-home-6.2.878688.c0ffb9674d.
30  Amandla Thomas-Johnson, "Nearly 100 Trinidadians Held at Al-Hol Camp in Northern Syria," *Middle-East Eye*, November 15, 2019: https://www.middleeasteye.net/news/revealed-nearly-100-trinidadians-held-al-hol-camp-northern-syria.
31  Hubbard, "In a Crowded Syria Tent Camp, the Women and Children of ISIS Wait in Limbo."
32  See "I WANT TO COME HOME: MOTHER IMPRISONED IN SYRIA WRITES TO FAMILY MEMBERS," *Alert T&T*, November 26, 2018: https://www.facebook.com/alertTandT/posts/i-want-to-come-home-mother-imprisoned-in-syria-writes-to-family-members-relative/338277500088703/.
33  See Jonathan Shaub, "Hoda Muthana and Shamima Begum: Citizenship and Expatriation in the U.S. and U.K.," *Lawfare*, February 25, 2019: https://www.lawfareblog.com/hoda-muthana-and-shamima-begum-citizenship-and-expatriation-us-and-uk.

34 See Azard Ali, "Trini ISIS Fighter Captured," *T&T Newsday*, February 5, 2019: https://newsday.co.tt/2019/02/05/trini-isis-fighter-captured/.
35 See Alexander, "Serious Threat to T&T."
36 Personal correspondence, July 24, 2017.
37 Cook and Vale, "From Daesh to 'Diaspora'," p. 15.
38 See Nalinee Seelal, "4 Trini ISIS Fighters Held," *T&T NEWSDAY*, January 19, 2016: http://archives.newsday.co.tt/2016/01/19/4-trini-isis-fighters-held/.
39 See "Trinis Detained at Iraqi Camp," *T&T Guardian*, January 13, 2018: http://www.guardian.co.tt/news/2018-01-12/trinis-detained-iraqi-camp.
40 Ensor, "Foreign Wives and Widows Face Conveyor-belt Justice in Iraqi Courts after the Defeat of Islamic State."
41 See "Trinis Deported from Turkey under Probe," *Trinidad and Tobago Guardian*, April 30, 2017: http://www.guardian.co.tt/news/2017-04-29/trinis-deported-turkey-under-probe.
42 Interview: Abu Sa'd at-Trinidadi," p. 69.
43 Robin Simcox, "European Islamist Plots and Attacks since 2014—and How the U.S. Can Help Prevent Them," The Heritage Foundation, August 1, 2017: https://www.heritage.org/sites/default/files/2017-08/BG3236.pdf.
44 Julien Neaves, "Young: No TT Citizens Confirmed at Syrian Refugee Camp," *T&T Newsday*, July 3, 2019: https://newsday.co.tt/2019/07/03/young-no-tt-citizens-confirmed-at-syrian-refugee-camp/.
45 Julien Neaves, "Suffering TT Children in Syria Will Freeze to Death," *T&T Newsday*, November 18, 2019: https://newsday.co.tt/2019/11/18/suffering-tt-children-in-syria-will-freeze-to-death/.
46 Norimitsu Onishi and Elian Peltier, "Turkey's Deportations Force Europe to Face Its ISIS Militants," *The New York Times*, November 18, 2019: https://www.nytimes.com/2019/11/17/world/europe/turkey-isis-fighters-europe.html.
47 Kevon Felmine, "Imam Claims Women, Children Not War Criminals," *T&T Guardian*, July 2, 2019: https://guardian.co.tt/news/imam-claims-women-children-not-war-criminals-6.2.877952.d3904cf8de.
48 Jensen La Vende, "Anti-Terrorism Act Now Law," *T&T Newsday*, August 20, 2018: https://newsday.co.tt/2018/08/20/anti-terrorism-act-now-law/.
49 https://www.unodc.org/documents/treaties/Special/2000_Protocol_to_Prevent_2C_Suppress_and_Punish_Trafficking_in_Persons.pdf.

50  See Mia Bloom, "How the Islamic State Recruits and Coerces Children," *The Conversation*, August 23, 2016: http://theconversation.com/how-the-islamic-state-recruits-and-coerces-children-64285.
51  See "Child Soldiers Become Integral Part of ISIS' Army," *CBS News*, November 23, 2014: https://www.cbsnews.com/news/child-soldiers-become-integral-part-of-isis-army/
52  See Josh Halliday, "Female Jihadis Publish Guide to Life under Islamic State," *The Guardian*, February 5, 2015: https://www.theguardian.com/world/2015/feb/05/jihadist-girl-marry-liberation-failed-islamic-state.
53  Lindsey Hilsum, "Captured ISIS Member Says He Just Wants to Go Home," *Channel 4 News*, March 6, 2019: https://www.channel4.com/news/captured-isis-member-says-he-just-wants-to-go-home.

# Conclusion

1  For a critique of this explanatory trope, see esp. James A. Piazza, "Rooted in Poverty?: Terrorism, Poor Economic Development, and Social Cleavages," *Terrorism & Political Violence* 18 (1) (2006), pp. 159–77.
2  See Lawrence Wright, *The Looming Tower* (London: Allen Lane, 2007), pp. 304–5.
3  Olivier Roy, *Jihad and Death: The Global Appeal of Islamic State* (London: Hurst, 2017).
4  In his research on foreign fighters in Iraq in 2005, Alan B. Krueger contends that low levels of civil liberties helped drive foreign fighter recruitment in that country (see Alan B. Krueger, "The National Origins of Foreign Fighters in Iraq" (Unpublished Manuscript, Princeton University, 2006)).
5  Efraim Benmelech and Esteban F. Klor, "What Explains the Flow of Foreign Fighters to ISIS?," *Terrorism & Political Violence* (2018), DOI:10.1080/09546553.2018.1482214, p. 2.
6  Ibid., p.20.
7  Ibid., p. 3.
8  William McCants and Christopher Meserole, "The French Connection," *Foreign Affairs*, March 24, 2016: https://www.foreignaffairs.com/articles/2016-03-24/french-connection.

9   Stephen Bullivant and Michael Ruse (eds.), *The Oxford Handbook of Atheism* (Oxford: Oxford University Press, 2016), p. 603.
10  See Nasser Mustafa, "New Organizations in Trinidad and Tobago," in *The Encyclopedia of Caribbean Religions: Volume 1*, edited by Patrick Taylor and Frederick I. Case (Chicago: University of Illinois University Press, 2013), p. 401.
11  Moamen Gouda and Marcus Marktanner hypothesize that youth unemployment is the driving determinant of foreign fighter recruitment to ISIS (Moamen Gouda and Marcus Marktanner, "Muslim Youth Unemployment and Expat Jihadism: Bored to Death?," *Studies in Conflict & Terrorism* 42 (10) (2019).
12  Sally Chidzoy and David Keller, "Luton Family of 12 'May Have Gone to Syria'," *BBC News*, July 1, 2015: https://www.bbc.co.uk/news/uk-england-beds-bucks-herts-33347117.
13  Vikram Dodd and Nadia Khomami, "Luton Family of 12 Feared to Have Gone to Syria," *The Guardian*, July 1, 2015: https://www.theguardian.com/world/2015/jul/01/luton-family-of-12-feared-gone-syria.
14  See Jay Akbar, "'All 12 of Us Are in the Islamic State': Luton Family Confirm they ARE in Syria and Encourage Other Britons to Join Them," *Mail Online*, July 4, 2015: http://www.dailymail.co.uk/news/article-3149190/All-12-Islamic-State-Luton-family-release-statement-confirming-Syria.html.
15  On the existential attractions of terrorism, see Simon Cottee and Keith Hayward, "Terrorist (E)motives: The Existential Attractions of Terrorism," *Studies in Conflict & Terrorism* 34 (2011), pp. 963–86.
16  George Orwell, *The Collected Essays, Journalism and Letters, Volume 2*, edited by Ian Angus and Sonia Orwell (London: Penguin, 1993).
17  See "TT Imam Supports Afghans against US," *The T&T Express*, September 18, 2001.
18  See https://www.facebook.com/permalink.php?story_fbid=2015842798632517&id=100006204490363.
19  Quoted in Joan Rampersad, "Nafeesa Condemns Wahabi Movement," *T&T Newsday*, October 19, 2018: https://newsday.co.tt/2018/10/18/nafeesa-condemns-wahabi-movement-wants-meaningful-dialogue-on-tt-families-in-syria/.

20  On the importance of local dynamics in foreign fighter mobilization, see Nate Rosenblatt and David Sterman, *All Jihad Is Local*, Vol. 3, April 2018, New America: https://www.newamerica.org/international-security/policy-papers/all-jihad-local-volume-ii/.
21  See Marc Sageman, *Understanding Terror Networks* (Philadelphia: University of Pennsylvania Press, 2004); Sageman, *Leaderless Jihad*; Sean C. Reynolds and Mohammed M. Hafez, "Social Network Analysis of German Foreign Fighters in Syria and Iraq," *Terrorism and Political Violence*, 2017, DOI: 10.1080/09546553.2016.1272456; Timothy Holman, "'Gonna Get Myself Connected': The Role of Facilitation in Foreign Fighter Mobilizations," *Perspectives on Terrorism* 10 (2) (2016), pp. 2–23.
22  See https://lyrics.fandom.com/wiki/The_Mighty_Sniper:Portrait_Of_Trinidad.

# Further Reading

Daniel Byman, *Road Warriors: Foreign Fighters in the Armies of Jihad* (New York: Oxford University Press, 2019).

Colin P. Clarke, *After the Caliphate: The Islamic State & the Future Terrorist Diaspora* (Cambridge: Polity Press, 2019).

Simon Cottee, *ISIS and the Pornography of Violence* (New York: Anthem, 2019).

Ramesh Deosaran, *A Society under Siege* (St. Augustine: University of the West Indies Press, 1997).

Daurius Figueira, *Jihad in Trinidad and Tobago, July 27, 1990* (Lincoln, NE: Writers Club Press, 2002).

Patrick French, *The World Is What It Is: The Authorized Biography of V.S. Naipaul* (London: Picador, 2008).

Phil Gurski, *Western Foreign Fighters: The Threat to Homeland and International Security* (London: Roman & Littlefield, 2017).

Thomas Hegghammer, *The Caravan: Abdallah Azzam And The Rise of Global Jihad* (Cambridge: Cambridge University Press, 2020).

Alexander Meleagrou-Hitchens, *Incitement: Anwar al-Awlaki's Western Jihad* (Cambridge, Mass: Harvard University Press, 2020).

V.S. Naipaul, *The Return of Eva Perón* (New York: Alfred A. Knopf, 1980).

V.S. Naipaul, *The Middle Passage: Impressions of Five Colonial Societies* (London: Picador, 1996).

Raoul A. Pantin, *Days of Wrath: The 1990 Coup in Trinidad and Tobago* (Lincoln, NE: iUniverse, 2007).

Graeme Wood, *The Way of the Strangers: Encounters with the Islamic State* (London: Penguin, 2017).

# Index

Abdul Haqq, Aliya 32, 33–5, 105, 109
Abdul Haqq, Tariq 31–3, 34–6, 39
Abdullah, Bilaal 30, 66, 67
Abdullah, Umar 59, 64–5, 66, 83, 114, 129
Adnani, Abu Muhammad al- 38, 55
Agard, Lennox 9
Aleong, Eddie 49
Alexander, Aleem 79
Algernon, Milton 2, 10, 12, 14–16, 38, 41, 50, 66–8, 72, 74, 79, 83
Ali, Emraan 49, 65
Ali, Zainool 50
Amis, Martin 3
Amriki, Abu Isa al- 74–84
Amriki, Umm Isa al- 74–6
Anyabwile, Hasan 121, 124, 125, 129
Atiba, Kwesi 22, 129
Aubaida, Zaki 27
Awlaki, Anwar al- 34

Bakr, Fuad Abu 18, 19, 29, 30, 86, 87, 129
Bakr, Yasin Abu 5, 17, 18, 19–30, 50, 59, 66–7, 87, 123, 129
Bassant, Mark 79, 92
Browne, Ryan 93

Callimachi, Rukmini 77, 98
Charles, Rodney 87
Choate, Ashmead 14, 16, 83, 125
Christopher Clarke, Warren 98
Cook, Peter 76
Crawford, Joan 8–17
Crawford, Shane 2–3, 7–18, 38, 39, 41, 45, 47, 50, 56, 68, 72, 74, 78–9, 82–3, 86, 113, 125

*Dabiq* 2, 7, 8, 13–17, 39, 78–9, 82–3, 113, 132
Deosaran, Ramesh 25
Dillon, Edmund 71, 88, 92, 108, 113

Elder, Pamela 32
Entenmann, Eva 37, 40
Es, Ana van 98–100

Faisal, Abdullah el- 45–6, 66, 124–5
Farrakhan, Louis 101
Ferreira, Abebe Oboi 106, 109
Figueira, Daurius 29, 30, 66, 81–2, 114, 125, 129
Francois, Susan 85
Fraser, Mark 7

Gaddafi, Muammar 29, 67
Ginkel, Bibi van 37, 40
Gold, Danny 28
Greene, Abbey 32
Griffith, Gary 84, 90–2, 117, 129

Hamid, Zaid Abdul 14, 31, 44–5, 47, 93, 98, 101, 112
Hamlet, Anthony 79, 98–9, 105, 112

Ibrahim, Kareem 8, 27

Jackman, Michael 92

Kallipersad, Dominic 22
Kareem, Abdul 24

Lee, Nicholas Joseph 112
Lewis, Chris 33, 50, 74, 79
Luqman, Chinonesu 86
Luqman, Jamelia 10, 12, 41

Madeira, Jones 28
Mahabir, Cynthia 51
Malchan, Joel 1, 78
McKernan, Bethan 106–7
Miles, Gene 21
Mohamed, Stuart 2, 15–16, 38, 50, 68, 72, 74, 77, 79–81, 83
Mohammad, Shadi Jabar Khalil 76
Mohammed, Nafeesa 86–7, 126
Mohammed, Nazim 2, 30, 33, 41, 48–51, 53–69, 72–3, 82–3, 98, 113, 123–5, 127, 129
Mohammed, Shazam 93, 101
Mohammed, Ziyad 44, 112
Moonilal, Roodal 3, 88
Muhammad, Nuru 109–10, 153
Muhammad, Osyaba 33
Muslimeen, Jamaat al- (JAM) 5, 8, 17, 19–30, 51, 66, 121

Pantin, Raoul 20, 21, 23, 25, 28–9, 57, 61, 130
Parson, Sean 45–7, 80, 143
Perkins-Ferreira, Felicia 106–11
Persad-Bissessar, Kamla 2, 12, 13

Ramirez, Tricia 101–5, 109
Ramlogan, Anand 27
Rasheed, Salim 27
Rawi, Faris al- 17, 85, 87, 95
Roach, Marvin 97, 101–6, 108–9, 123
Roach, Muhammad 101–5
Roach, Qadirah 101–5
Robinson, Arthur 20, 21, 26
Rowley, Keith 88, 94–5, 106
Ryan, Selwyn 22–3

Sageman, Marc 13, 36, 39
Schmitt, Eric 98
Seetahal, Dana 27, 91
Shukrijumah, Adnan el- 50
Simcox, Robin 113
Sookdeo, Dharmendra 1, 78
Special Branch 59, 89–90, 117, 129
Stafford Smith, Clive 107–9
Starr, Barbara 93
Stephen, Wendell 29
Strategic Services Agency 54, 89, 117
Su, Gailon 97–100, 112
Su, Sarah Lee 98–9
Su, Su-lay 98–101
Sudani, Abu Sa'ad al- 76, 81
Surtees, Joshua 106–7, 130

Taylor, Dennis 24–5
Thomas, Barrington "Skippy" 12
Thomas, Keonna 46
Thomas-Johnson, Amandla 111
Todenhöfer, Jürgen 31, 36
Trinidadi, Abu Sa'd at- 7, 8, 15, 18
Trump, Donald 29, 31, 94

Vignes, Leo des 20

Waheed, Aneesa 33–4, 48, 53–61, 65, 73, 113
Waheed, Daud 48, 55–6, 65, 113
Waters, Roger 107
Williams, Eric 21, 24, 136

Young, Stuart 108–9

Zambelis, Chris 51
Zoellner, Tom 91

www.ingramcontent.com/pod-product-compliance
Ingram Content Group UK Ltd.
Pitfield, Milton Keynes, MK11 3LW, UK
UKHW020820240326
469204UK00019B/121